THE SPORTING ROAD

Also by Jim Fergus

One Thousand White Women
A Hunter's Road

THE
SPORTING

*Travels Across
America in an
Airstream
Trailer—with Fly
Rod, Shotgun,
and a Yellow Lab
Named Sweetzer*

Jim Fergus

ROAD

ST. MARTIN'S PRESS
New York

THE SPORTING ROAD. Copyright © 1999 by Jim Fergus. Introduction copyright © 1999 by Rick Bass. All rights reserved. Printed in the United States of America. No part of this book may be used or reproduced in any manner whatsoever without written permission except in the case of brief quotations embodied in critical articles or reviews. For information, address St. Martin's Press, 175 Fifth Avenue, New York, NY 10010.

All photographs copyright © 1999 by Stephen Collector

Library of Congress Cataloging-in-Publication Data

Fergus, Jim.
    The sporting road : travels across America in an airstream trailer, with fly rod, shotgun, and a yellow lab named Sweetzer / Jim Fergus.—1st ed.
        p.   cm.
    ISBN 0-312-24245-X
    1. Hunting—United States.   2. Fishing—United States.   I. Title.
SK41.F4   1999
799'.0973—dc21   99–15930
                                                                        CIP

First Edition: October 1999

Design by James Sinclair

10 9 8 7 6 5 4 3 2 1

CONTENTS

To David Christian, Stephen Collector, John Warner, David Wilhelm, and Jon Williams—old friends, boon companions

ACKNOWLEDGMENTS

I owe a great debt of gratitude to Brendan Banahan, who first offered me the opportunity to write the stories that became the seeds of this book. And in making that "small world" connection, thanks to my old childhood chums Julie and Jeff Ward. Special thanks to my loyal friend Oliver Moore, who kept me on at the magazine through thick and thin, until he himself was gone. Thanks to George Bell and Bob Brown who also let me hang my field editor hat there for a while.

I thank my artist friend Walt Spitzmiller, whose beautiful paintings illustrated many of these stories. I wish they could have been here, too, Walt. And thanks to my old partner in sport, Steve Collector, for the many beautiful photographs that have graced others of these stories in various publications, and that grace this book.

Thanks to Terry McDonell who gave me a new home at *Sports Afield* magazine and particularly to John Atwood, who let me move into my own room there. And to my man Dave

Scroppo, a very talented young editor at the magazine, and to Sarah Parsons, who makes me laugh—thanks, too.

Thanks to Doug Truax, my friend and editor at the All-Outdoors.com Web site for giving me a second, cyber home on the internet magazine *Jeep ® Sporting Destinations.*

Thanks to Becky Koh who signed this book up, and to Greg Cohn, who inherited it. Both made it better than it would have been.

Finally, thanks to the dozens of people, friends and acquaintances, with whom I have been afield during this past decade, who have extended their hospitality to me, given me an electric outlet in which to plug in the Airstream, shared hunting and fishing spots, fine meals, fine wine, and fine sport. Thank you all very much.

AUTHOR'S NOTE

Some version of many of the following stories first appeared in a column called "The Sporting Road," which I wrote between February 1994 and February 1997. Other stories, though written for the column, never ran for one reason or another and are published here for the first time. A number of the stories included here were originally published in *Sports Afield* magazine, others in *Jeep ® Sporting Destinations* on the All Outdoors Web site.

Many of these stories have been expanded or changed from their first publication—some to the extent that they barely resemble the original any longer. Sometimes only an idea or a paragraph survived and, as ideas and paragraphs have a way of doing, located other like-minded ideas and paragraphs to become new stories altogether. Still other stories are all new, written specifically for this collection. In some cases, the author has taken certain fictional liberties. Some names have been changed, and certain characters and situations altered or disguised in the

interest of preserving the privacy of various individuals or of protecting specific locales.

Finally, as this book represents a kind of extended six-year-long journey around the country, it has been arranged more or less seasonally and, like the successive seasons themselves, tends to overlap upon itself, so that one September runs into the next, and the next and the next. The sporting life is just like that.

THE SPORTING ROAD

A Good Hunting Partner
by Rick Bass

Generally I like dogs—my dogs or anyone's dogs—better than people, but Jim Fergus is different. I'm lucky to have him as a hunting partner, luckier still to have him as a friend, and for once I'm smart enough to know it. Or maybe I'm not as smart as I think I am; maybe I've got it backward, and a good hunting partner is harder to find than a good friend.

It doesn't matter. He's both. It's been one of the great curses of my life to be saddled with a love for pointing dogs, especially big-running, knot-headed German shorthairs, which are always breaking my heart by running off and vanishing or being shot by honyocks or—well, any of the thousands of tortures and heartbreaks that German shorthairs will inflict upon you.

Fergus is the one I call when my dogs run away or expire. He's the one who understands most clearly the awful, wonderful dependency we place upon them: the way they become reposi-

1

tories, over time, for our hopes and imagination; the way they instruct us in the manners of the world. The way they hunt—each dog adapting his or her specific style and character to fit the landscape and the quarry's, and no matter whether in the beginning we, the owners, perceive one of those characteristics to be a weakness, by the time the dog has aged some and grown to love us and we have grown to love the dog that flaw has become a strength.

Who knows where the transformation occurs? The dog has done nothing but keep loving us, and has endured. The change occurs in our own hearts. We grow to need them—not for leading us to game, meat, sport, but for how they soften our dying, too-angry hearts. When a hunter loses a dog, he or she is naked to the world. You never look at the autumn, or hunting, the same again.

Jim's the one I call, and talk to about it, whenever it happens.

A couple of years ago I had lost my great young Colter—a solid liver-colored, slashing field trail champ, and a sweet boy to boot. He would sleep spooned up with me in the bed in hotel rooms with his head on a pillow: a dog that had no quit in him, a dog like a dream. . . .

Someone had shot Colter, but I didn't know that: I didn't find his body for about six months. In the meantime I was sinking, falling, tumbling further beneath the world daily. Jim performed that hardest of tasks, during the time that I was hanging; he would call in periodically to see if there was any good news (knowing all the while that there wasn't, else he would have heard from me) and check to see how I was doing.

Colter had disappeared in September. That October, I hauled my depressed ass over to eastern Washington to make a hunt with Jim and a couple of his friends, Doug Tate and Tom Crawford. My heart wasn't in it, but Jim wanted me to go—wanted

me to bring my young pointers, Colter's brothers two years his junior, and take my medicine.

I knew I'd be a damp blanket over the party, and Jim and his friends knew it. They invited me nonetheless, knowing I needed to get out there and begin again. The season passes quickly. You can rest a sad heart but not a young dog.

The four of us camped in an old log cabin high in the mountains, with all of our dogs—French Brittanys, Labs, Betty-dog, and the two wild pointers, the Asshole Brothers, Pointman and Superman—and each morning we drove down into the Palouse prairie to hunt, hunting a different species each day: chukars in and along the basalt cliffs and rubble, Huns in the gold wheat stubble, California quail in the oak and poison sumac creek bottoms, and wheat-fat pheasants in the hills and draws. Our friend Guy had hoped to make the hunt but had health problems come up at the last moment, though he sent a case of wine for us. (It's the thought that counts, but I might as well mention, it was a tremendous wine, far beyond anything we would have gotten for ourselves or even our friends.)

I was there in the prairies and mountains with them for several days. I remember only a handful of images, a mosaic of dull, slow healing. I remember smiling and laughing even when there was an awful hollowness and sadness in me, and I remember Jim knowing it was that way for me but saying nothing, knowing that the medicine required was to keep on going. I would look at Jim and the others, healthy and carefree and in full possession of their dogs, their whole business. The life of a hunter. The world so alive in October, while you're hunting, that some days, in some moments, it's like a kind of overstimulation: as if your body gets outside your skin.

A fine retrieve of a crippled Hun by my liver Superman, while the other hunters stood on a cliff two hundred feet above and watched like spectators in the bleachers as he hunted it down in the tall grass, found it, pointed it again, then caught and

retrieved it; eighty-degree heat, a fifteen-minute search, and the calls and murmurs began to drift down, *"That bird's not there. . . ."*

Stopping to eat wild plums at an old abandoned homestead. Hunting quail down in the blazing red and gold foliage of creek bottoms, hunters clattering across cobblestone, quail rising and buzzing all around as if riding on a carnival, up and down through the oak canopy, little circus birds, puffs of blue smoke from the guns, some of the quail falling, my dogs busting coveys ahead of us, wings whirring we never saw, pointer yips and yelps, and no one saying anything, no one really minding, it's just the way some days, many days, go. . . .

One evening, perhaps sensing my lost-dog thoughts, Jim commented to all of us, "You know, it seems like it should be the other way around, but I never remember a bad thing my dog ever did, or a good shot I made. I always remember the great flushes and my missed shots." And that seemed to me, and seems, to state perfectly how a hunter puts the land and his dogs and his quarry always before him, never behind or beneath. . . .

All those dogs, all those friends. Not a single lost bird in five days. Great meals in the evenings. Book talk, sure, yeah. Brown Superman, like a chunkier ghost of Colter, staunch on Huns in the gold stubble beneath purple evening storm banks; the sight soothing something in me, the dog staunch as a carved-stone statue, some archetype of relaxation being struck within me, sorrow slowly dissolving, and Jim coming up afterward and bragging on my dog. . . .

That was the day Doug Tate shot all four species in a day—he got the Hun at fifty yards at dusk in storm light as the rest of us were all already sitting on the tailgate, end-of-day-watching, again not as participants but like an audience. . . .

I am not saying hunters have to always hunt to feel most fully alive. I am not saying that too often we watch life, instead of getting out and living it. What I am trying to get at with these

memories is that with a good friend, a good hunting partner, the two things—watching and doing—are about the same. And it's not that way for much else in the world.

I remember a grouse hunt I made with Jim up in the Yaak, my rainy, snowy home in northwest Montana. We hunted for three good hours in a steady cold rain, wisps of steam and fog rising from the drenched woods, back in the days of Colter. Sweetz was as luminous as butter, moving through those dark woods, whereas Colter was nearly invisible, even when he was within range, which wasn't often. We found perhaps three birds in those three hours, one shot was fired, a clean miss, and I toweled off my old gun and then waited and watched with admiration and pleasure as Jim took the time to disassemble and completely oil and clean his gun, storing it in the little briefcase in which it would fit, broken apart: a neat end to an untidy day, muddy, happy, wet dogs tail-thumping around our ankles and the rain still coming down. . . . I'm trying to learn that kind of neatness from Jim, though it's a tough lesson. The way he babies his beloved dogs: he's always solicitous of their feet, their thirst, their hunger. I'm trying to learn that, as well. Trying to learn *manners* from him. My own are considerably looser; I tend to push my dogs, my equipment, myself, too hard, too sloppily, spilling over, *pushing*.

So it's established, I hope, that he's caring. And neat. But truth be told, actually, sometimes he's a bit beyond neat. I would never dare use the term *prissy*—he's polite, courteous, solicitous even with assholes all the way up to some distant point (but, buddy, once that point is crossed, he'll cut the offender up verbally with the most wicked observation, always all the more effective for its brutal truth)—but still, he's, well, *neat*. It fascinates me; I admire it.

Cocktails come every day at first dark. They are a part of his

hunts, a mechanism of the day's hunt as surely as the ejectors on a shotgun or the hemostats in the vest. A component: everything in its place.

Something he won't tell you about in these essays is that every morning, inside the gleaming aluminum hull of his Airstream, that orderly ship of dreams, the vessel that has hauled great hearted Sweetz and sweet, cheerful, friendly Betty the nonhunter, and now the sassy, talented genius Henri, the continuous groin licker (his own, not others,) across the many years and miles, is that Jim will eat Honey Nut Cheerios for breakfast.

Every morning it's the same. He arises early, lets the dogs out, fixes coffee, reads or works, eats Honey Nut Cheerios. Routine, amid a variance, a diversity, of seasons and landscapes and hunts.

No one is perfect. There is always some dirt, some secret.

As you read these essays—including his description of a hunt in Nebraska on horseback, as he follows the rise and fall through the grass swales—the thought might occur that here is a man who belongs intensely in the West. But then you will come upon his description of a day spent fishing in the mud-brown of the South—his utter delight in it—and you might think, for a moment, that no, you were mistaken; here is a man who belongs intensely in the swamps and pine woods.

Soon enough, however, you understand. The common denominator is not geographical, but internal: here is a man who belongs intensely to the living.

And slowly, gradually—essay by essay—you become aware of the unsaid: the fact that he fits a diminishing time, a diminishing space, and a diminishing code of manners. That he always puts others before him; that he considers and respects his friends, his prey, his dogs, and the landscapes that engage these things.

You become aware, too, that there is less and less time and space in which he can be quiet and live his life by this code of considerate manners, living his life as the stars call for him to live it. Autumn, however, is surely when he has his best shot at

it, and perhaps this is one of the most telling indicators of a great hunting partner: that you don't have to always, or even often, hunt with him. Once you have such a friend, you can hear secondhand of a hunt he or she made solo, or with others elsewhere, and share the pleasure, the specifications, of it vicariously.

You can imagine the rain dimpling the tin roof of the Airstream and the dogs slumbering and a man reading by flashlight or up late working by battery light. You can imagine coffee brewing in the morning—the smell of it—and the dogs awakening, some stiff and old but full of memories, but others young and goofy and hungry for the world. You can imagine a world waiting to be inhabited fully and a man stepping forward into it, day after day, neatly, and stepping into that world with an utter, awed respect, and an observance, which often crosses over into wonder.

You'll see. The pages that follow are almost like the real thing, almost like being there.

Of Dogs and Shotguns/Wives and Furniture

> *He was a huntsman of renown,*
> *He was a man about the town,*
> *He shot, he fished, his bag he filled;*
> *He hawked and talked and lady killed.*

> —Micheal Brander,
> *"On the Trail of Colonel Thorton"*

Well, OK, so I'm not actually a hawker ... or, truth be told (as it will here), a lady-killer. I am neither a huntsman of renown nor a man about the town; rarely do I fill my bag. Hell, I'm not even much of a talker. For that matter, I don't really see how hawking and lady-killing ever got into the same line of bad verse. Somehow I guess the latter activity must have been considered by the Georgian British to be all one with the manly pursuits of fishing and hunting. Which seems odd to me, as

8

many of my most obsessive male sporting friends and acquaintances have more or less had to give up the companionship of the opposite sex altogether, because they simply can't fit "lady-killing" into their busy sporting lives.

There's my painter friend Len Chmiel, for instance, twice divorced, who puts it this way: "I finally decided that you have a choice in life between dogs and shotguns, and wives and furniture, and I've opted for the dogs and shotguns." A remark which might certainly be viewed by some as a bit hard-line, possibly even misogynistic. But then that's Len's business.

For my part, I tend to look at the activities of hunting and fishing and of time spent wandering around in the outdoors in general somewhat in the manner of chemical paint strippers that, when troweled over our everyday lives, begin to bubble and blister and peel away the dead layers—the viscous gunk of existence—exposing finally, if not exactly pure epiphany, at least a relatively clean surface.

And then I think of my father, who died when he was only fifty-seven years old, less than a decade from now in my own life span, and who did himself in by sitting in his leather easy chair sucking on Camels and drinking Dewar's, watching television and reading the newspaper, which was Pop's way of sedating and insulating himself from the not inconsiderable heartbreaks of his own life.

I am, after all, my father's son, and one day a few years ago, feeling unusually flush, I went out and bought myself a leather easy chair with a matching ottoman—just like Pop had when I was a kid. Damn, it was comfortable! After having been sent by a magazine on a six-day press junket to Scotland to tour whisky distilleries, I had developed, I am sorry to confess, a late-blooming taste for scotch whisky. I had even begun flirting again with the evil dreaded Camels, which I had given up some years before.

Of course, we all know the truth in the old saw about becoming more like our parents as we grow older, but I hadn't

been around Pop since I turned sixteen (on which dark day I was at least partly responsible for his death), and so I hardly saw how he could be having much influence on me now. I guess it was just the old family genes rearing their ugly heads, and although the thought did not exactly hit me like a ton of bricks, neither did it escape my attention that I was in grave danger of gradually (or possibly not so gradually) becoming Pop—solitary and withdrawn, with a Pop-like potbelly. I was even getting grouchy like Pop. Some of my friends had taken to calling me Grampy behind my back.

Meanwhile, my faithful yellow Lab, Sweetzer, had actually taken to carrying my slippers around in her mouth. Sweetz wasn't getting any younger herself. She had congenitally bad elbows and by age six had already undergone two surgeries and was currently being treated by a canine acupuncturist. Like an aging professional athlete, Sweetz was thickening a bit around the middle and sometimes walked stiffly on her damaged joints— and maybe she couldn't play the whole game anymore, but she still had some great innings left in her.

Other clear indicators notwithstanding, you know it's time to hit the road again when your wife gives you a "personal grooming device" (aka an ear and nose hair trimmer) as a gift for your forty-fifth birthday and, what's more, it's exactly what you wanted.

Certainly, there are plenty of other good reasons and/or valid excuses for this life of sport (not the least of them being that it's my job). My wife, who had a grown son from a previous marriage, and I had decided early on not to have children of our own. I mention this only because it would be difficult indeed for an attentive father (and hardly a wealthy one at that) to be touring the countryside with gun and dog and fishing rod. Better not to be a parent at all than to be a bad parent (which advice is the full extent of what I know about parenthood). It's difficult enough for an attentive husband to slip out of the house re-

peatedly and for prolonged periods as I have managed to do for the better part of the past decade.

Recently, in the course of my travels, I found myself sitting around an anonymous motel room in an anonymous small town in the Great Plains with my hunting companions of the day—Bill, Patrick, Butch, and Douglas. We had made a successful sharptail grouse hunt that day and had just finished a delicious game bird dinner that we'd cooked ourselves in my Airstream trailer, in which I was camped behind the motel, and on a camp stove in front of the room. Like me, these fellows spend enough time in rural America to have learned that it's best to pack along your own cooking gear in order to avoid a steady diet of middle-American road food, which, literally, will eventually kill you.

The dogs were sleeping soundly on their dog beds, exhausted from the day's hunt, and the hunters were in various postures, seated or reclined on the motel beds, propped up by pillows, when the conversation, as it occasionally does, turned to the matter of marriage and sport: "How does your wife feel about you being on the road all the time?" I was asked—a common-enough question.

To which I gave my standard nonanswer: "It's my job."

A few years ago, in a review of a book I wrote called *A Hunter's Road*, a critic in the *New York Times Book Review* speculated that my wife "must be an extraordinarily patient and indulgent woman to have put up with her husband's adolescent wandering and maiming of things." At the time I felt that this was a rather impertinent observation on the part of the critic and a remark that falls considerably beyond the bailiwick of book reviewing; such domestic matters are none of the critic's damn business. But I also know what he meant. Beyond the undeniable romance and sweet sentimentalities of fishing and wing shooting, beyond the elegance of fly rods and rising trout, the aesthetics of fine guns and noble gun dogs, beyond the esteemed history and venerable traditions of Sport, with a capital

S, lies something that our spouses, especially if they themselves are nonhunters and nonfisherpersons, have suspected all along: we're just great big kids, perpetually trying to yank some scaly creature or other from the depths of the water or chasing some small helpless "handful of feathers" (as my pal Guy de la Valdène puts it in his lovely book of that name) around the countryside with our dogs and shotguns, all the while trying to delude ourselves and others (especially our families) into believing that such pursuits are actually quite important. What no one ever wants to admit, especially in print, is that often these activities are just plain fun, providing, as the Spanish philosopher Ortega y Gasset put it, "a vacation from the human condition." Indeed, such a concept is so uncomplicated that it hardly seems to require the services of a philosopher. Nor, I believe, should any man or woman ever have to apologize for it.

On the other hand, I tend to think of those of us who are in the distinctly peculiar position of making our living, or some portion thereof, by "vacationing" from the human condition as being kind of like old Sitting Bull (if slightly less heroic), who probably never had to explain to Mrs. Sitting Bull why he and the boys were going out hunting again. If the great Sitting Bull didn't go out hunting he'd be considered a total deadbeat. His family would be poor and hungry and dressed in handouts supplied by families whose men were hunters. So even on those days when maybe Sitting Bull felt like sleeping in, lounging around on the buffalo robes in his warm lodge, and skipping the day's hunt altogether, there was the formidable Mrs. Sitting Bull getting her husband's hunting outfit together, collecting his bow and arrows, sending the horse boy to bring in his best hunting pony, and then booting Sitting Bull's lazy ass right out of the tepee. *"Get out there,"* I imagine her commanding, *"and don't come home without a nice fat buffalo cow."* Which is kind of what my wife does.

And so I asked the other men that evening in the motel room

out in the middle of the plains (in the heart of the country that Sitting Bull himself used to hunt, these birds we had just eaten the descendants of the birds he probably hunted as a boy to hone his early skills) how their wives reacted to their own passion for sport, their frequent and prolonged absences. Patrick, a carpenter by trade, smiled wryly and said, "Actually, I'm in the middle of a divorce. So I guess she didn't care for it much." And everybody laughed, because what else is there to do? But certainly, failed marriages are not all that funny, and although I doubt that there are any statistics available on the subject, my guess is that the genetic predisposition of certain members of our species to pursue sport has resulted in its fair share of divorces in these times—and certainly in plenty of domestic discord. Nor is this intended to be a "boy's club" observation, as a reader of a sporting magazine I once worked for accused me in a letter to the editor. I am well aware that many husbands and wives enjoy active sporting lives together. It just seems to me that the primal urge to hunt and fish, long since given up by the vast majority of human beings as a requisite means of feeding and clothing one's family, is more often and more culturally correctly taken out these days in the workplace, by both men and women, where the old predatory instincts are more highly valued than ever. Which isn't quite the point of sport, either, is it?

So when I got home I asked my own wife why she felt that women sometimes resented their husband's sporting excursions. She thought it over for a while, and then she said, "Well, you're asking the wrong person, because, of course, *it's your job*. But I would say in general that if she's not interested herself in hunting and fishing, the wife might just get lonely. Maybe she wants her husband home doing some work around the house, and maybe she is a little jealous that he's off male-bonding with his buddies and they're all having so much fun without their wives. Or, if he happens to be hunting or fishing alone, that he's having

so much fun all alone, without her. I think it makes her feel left out—which is not to say that she wants to go along, because I, for one, don't."

"But that doesn't mean that husbands don't have a different kind of fun when they're at home with their wives," I argued. "And, you know, generally the chores do get done—sure, maybe it'll be next week or the week after that, but eventually they get done, and the men come home and go back to work and earn

their living, much refreshed from having had a little fun. It's like Ortega y Gasset said: 'When you are fed up with the troublesome present, with being 'very twentieth century,' you take your gun, whistle for your dog, go out to the mountain, and give yourself the pleasure during a few hours or a few days of being a hunter.' "

"Hey," laughed my wife, "you don't need to sell me. Remember, I'm the extraordinarily patient and indulgent woman who puts up with your adolescent wandering and maiming of things."

Yet another posthunt at the very end of a long bird season found me sitting around a campfire in the Arizona desert with a couple of artist friends—the aforementioned Len Chmiel, who is a superb painter not yet famous only because he refuses to live in New York and has so little talent for self-promotion (and because he spends so much time hunting), and Doug Baer, ditto, a master wildlife sculptor who also by choice lives out in the middle of the vast flyover country between LA and New York. Parked just beyond the ring of firelight were our vehicles—Len's '86 Ford van, Doug's '86 Suburban, and, at a mere ten years old, the latest model of the lot, my '87 Suburban. Collectively, these beat-up old workhorses represented nearly thirty years of driving and well over six hundred thousand miles—hard miles at that—logged by three wandering sportsmen whose paths happened to intersect out here in the desert in February at the tail end of the bird season.

Now we were sitting around the campfire having just finished yet another wonderful game dinner. We were sharing a bottle of wine and discussing the fact that by nearly any definition of modern society we might all be considered dismal failures. None of us earned much money by the standards of the world's economy, and we all still lived the rather hand-to-mouth existence of artists and writers and itinerant sporting bums. We were all still knocking around, scraping along, waiting for that next

check in the mail, which may or may not arrive. We all still drove rattletrap old vehicles with upholstery worn thin and impregnated forever with the unmistakable stink of dogs. We'd all known our fair measure of personal disaster and heartbreak (who hasn't?). Two out of three of us had been divorced; the third had gazed hard into the precipice. But here we were, with our dreams present and accounted for, if not exactly intact, and with prospects—or so, at least, we believed, for this is a faith central to our tribe.

Earlier we had hunted an area around Black Mountain. It had been a marginal bird year in the southwest, populations of Scaled and Gambel's quail determined almost entirely by the amount of rainfall the previous spring and summer, and we had worked hard for only a few birds. But that was alright for we were all walkers and could walk all day, one reason we enjoyed hunting together. In any case, the last day of bird season has a specific, bittersweet texture all its own and no one cares much about numbers. By then dogs are tired and beaten up, their paws sore from scrambling over the volcanic rock that spills from the draws, and from the ubiquitous prickly pear and cholla cactus. And the hunters themselves are worn a bit thin from the long season, and possibly even feel some sense of relief at its imminent close.

Notorious runners in any circumstances, the desert quail themselves are even more skittish than usual late in the season, dashing out ahead of the dogs, dodging past the cacti, or flying wild way out in front, proof of the old saw that you should hunt them in tracks and running shorts—were it not for the cacti.

Just at dusk, hunting alone with Sweetz, the sun setting over the Picacho mountains, she got birdy, trailing a running covey. I hurried to keep up, on one side of us a cholla jungle, oddly exotic, nearly tropical in the soft, pink evening light, and on the other side a dense thicket of mesquite and other thorny brush, into which the quail now ran, Sweetz in hot pursuit.

But I could not follow for the thickness of the cover, I could

only hear the musical whirring of wings of the escaping covey as she finally pushed them to flight and I thought this the perfect way to end the season, the wingbeats of next year's brood stock fading into the dusk.

Now sitting around the campfire, Len told a story about how he gave everything up to become a fine artist, about being down to his last twelve cents and a can of sauerkraut.

And Doug told a story about growing up in Montana's Yellowstone National Park, where one time as he boy he crawled into a hibernating grizzly bear den, the game being to "touch griz" and bring out a handful of hair as proof. His best friend lay at the den entrance just behind him, his job to grab hold of Doug's ankles and pull him out after he'd counted coup on the bear. But evidently the griz, not in full hibernation, woke up when Doug touched him, stirred and bellowed, and Doug called to his friend: "Pull me out! Pull me out!" But his friend, so terrified by the roar of the bear, was now running full tilt away from the den, leaving Doug all alone with the griz. Perhaps this story might serve as a useful metaphor for the artist's life.

"I just feel so lucky," Len said, staring into the fire, "to be out here, to be able to live the way we do." And the three of us agreed that we wouldn't trade our lives, dicey as they may have been, and still are, for anything else on this earth.

But I'm getting way ahead of myself now. That campfire lies near the end of the many seasons represented in these pages, comes at the end of a long road, a road that really has no end— and I don't mean to be cute about that. It just occurs to me that if, like Pop, we don't keep moving, we're dead. Maybe it's just as simple as that. Maybe that is the main point of sport— to stay on the move, to stay engaged, connected to the natural world in some more meaningful way than having one's butt attached to the seat of a leather easy chair.

And maybe it is a simple matter of escapism after all. We carry so much human baggage around all of our lives—sundry guilt and childhood traumas and anger, the deaths of loved ones,

various troubles and regrets, so many "what-ifs" and "should-haves" and "if onlys." *I should have called the ambulance sooner for Pop that morning of my sixteenth birthday, if only I had he probably wouldn't have died.* They don't necessarily incapacitate us, such things, but they weigh us down; we put them each in a box and store them away somewhere inside our broken hearts and carry them along for the rest of our lives. It is the "human condition" of which Ortega y Gassett speaks.

The beauty of the natural world, the state of grace offered by hunting and fishing, the pure focus of attention demanded by fish and game birds and dogs, and by the companions with whom we go afield, offers us such clear and uncluttered respite from our ghosts, allows us to lay down our little boxes for a while and infinitely lighten our souls. Is that not a good enough reason in itself to hunt and fish and wander the countryside?

So right now let's pretend it is barely daybreak . . . say, the first day of September, opening day of western bird season, which stretches out ahead like the seemingly endless summers of our youth; the Suburban is warming up in the driveway, the Airstream hooked up and ready to roll—its running lights glowing like those of a wingless aircraft in the milky light of dawn. Sweetz senses the beginning of the season, the excitement and promise of all that is to come, and as I dress she is whining and underfoot like a puppy, nuzzling me beneath my boxer shorts with an ice-cold nose (an old Lab trick that never fails to get my attention), and then picking shoes up off the floor, shaking them furiously between her teeth, as if she feels the need to make her existence further known to me lest I forget and leave home without her. Fat chance.

I finish dressing and load her in the back of the Suburban, where she collapses happily on her dog bed, sighs deeply, and promptly falls asleep. *Good*, she must be thinking as she dozes off. *The shoe thing worked again.*

And then I go in and kiss my half-asleep wife good-bye. She does not open her eyes but smiles slightly. She's seen me off so many times, and I think she knows that she'll have plenty of quality time in the future with her grumpy husband, in the seat of whose leather armchair she'll one day probably have to install an ejection button. But right now I am in the prime of my life and I have places to go, people to see, friends with whom to rendezvous, birds to roast, fish to fry, new country, and old, to visit. Yes, Sweetz and I have a job to do.

FALL

1

OPENING DAY

Perhaps too often the nonhunter might accuse the upland game sportsman of "killing off our birds," whatever the species might be. With the present controls on hunting this is, of course, utter nonsense. Far more important than the numbers of birds shot during the fall hunting season is the amount of winter food and cover available to support the survivors until the following breeding season.

—Paul A. Johnsgard, The Grouse of the World

It was opening day of grouse season in Colorado, and things just didn't feel right. For one thing, it was too hot to hunt, even in the high country where I live. But it wasn't only the weather; something else was clearly amiss. I had been dogged for several days by an impending sense of disaster, and then the day before the opener I was in Denver attending to some last-minute business before bird season when the Suburban broke down—I mean completely collapsed. I drove it limping and knocking, wheezing and smoking, groaning and leaking fluids from every orifice like

a great gut-shot beast into the shop, where, of course, because it was Friday, nothing could be done for it until the following week. "But tomorrow's opening day," I begged. "I've got a hunt scheduled. I'm meeting a friend; I need my vehicle."

The mechanic just shrugged, which is never a good sign. Clearly he wasn't a hunter and didn't give a damn about opening day.

So I went across the street to a car rental agency. It was hot as hell in the city, and naturally I was not in good mood. "I need a four-wheel-drive vehicle for the weekend," I said to the young rental agent.

"It's Labor Day weekend, sir," the agent replied with an unmistakable hint of reprimand in his voice. "I'm afraid we're completely out of four-wheel-drive vehicles."

"Great," I said. "Well, what about a truck, or even a van?"

He shook his head.

"A minivan?"

He shook his head.

"What do you have?"

"I can put you in a Ford Escort, sir," he said. "We have one left."

"A Ford Escort?" I said. "Tomorrow's opening day of bird season, and all you can give me to drive is a Ford Escort?" It was obvious to me that this fellow wasn't a hunter, either.

"Yes, sir, I'm afraid so. You won't find a four-wheel-drive vehicle to rent in the entire city this weekend. All the out-of-state tourists are going up to the mountains for Labor Day, and they all like to drive four-by-fours."

"But most of them never even leave the pavement," I said. "They don't need four-wheel drive."

"That may be, sir," the rental agent replied with a condescending smile, "but the tourists still like four-wheel-drive vehicles to get them to the mountains. It makes them feel like they're having an authentic Rocky Mountain experience."

"Yeah, well, I live here," I said, "and I'd also like to have an authentic Rocky Mountain experience."

"I'm very sorry, sir," he said, "but I'm afraid that for you, this weekend, that's just not going to happen."

"A Ford Escort . . . ," I muttered. "What the hell kind of a car is a Ford Escort for a field editor to be driving on opening day?"

"What's a field editor?" the young man asked.

I had to think about this for a minute. "I'm not sure," I finally admitted, "but I am one."

"Perhaps someone who edits in a field?" said the young fellow helpfully.

"Sure, that's it," I agreed. "Look; I'll take the Escort."

The next morning before dawn, I loaded Sweetz and my gear into the tiny subcompact and headed for Steamboat Springs, where I was meeting my friend Mike Mastro. Although the sun hadn't yet risen, it was already unseasonably warm, and now, driving in the Escort, it felt less than ever like opening day. I think even Sweetz was embarrassed by our new vehicle. She rode beside me in the front seat looking notably ungainly, too big for the little car, and somehow even dopier than Labs usually look.

Mastro has a brace of excellent little English springer spaniels whom he hunt-tests. He used to be a navigator for United Airlines, but then they transferred him to Newark, New Jersey. He lasted a week there before, like any self-respecting bird hunter faced with the prospect of bird season in Newark, he quit his job. Conveniently, this happened just before the season opened, and presently Mike was kind of dragging his heels about seeking new employment.

Mastro and I were looking for Columbian sharptail grouse (*Tympanuchus phasianellus columbianus*), of which there still exists a huntable population in this part of Colorado. Commonly

known as mountain sharptail, the bird is a slightly smaller sub-species of the more widely ranged plains sharptail. Sweetz and I had never hunted them before, but an acquaintance in the Division of Wildlife had suggested that if we intended to do so, we might want to get it done soon. Although populations of mountain sharptail in Colorado were considered to be generally stable, threatened and/or extirpated populations in neighboring states pointed to the distinct possibility that the subspecies might be reclassified as a separate species altogether and listed as threatened or endangered, in which case, of course, hunting them anywhere would no longer be allowed.

However, as Paul A. Johnsgard, perhaps the world's foremost expert on gallinaceous game birds, points out, the steady, tragic decline of this fine little bird has nothing whatsoever to do with hunting pressure, but with a complicated combination of factors that generally involve changing land use practices—overgrazing, fire suppression, "clean" farming, residential development, etc.

At the same time, further limiting hunting pressure on mountain sharptails in western Colorado (and hunting opportunities, as well) is the fact that most of the areas with the highest bird populations are on private land. The local landowners—ranchers, farmers, hobby ranchers, and second-home owners alike—tend to be protective of their sharptails, particularly where granting hunting access is concerned. Curiously, the parceling of the land into thirty-five-acre "ranchettes," the frequent destruction of sharptail nests while summer-fallowing wheat stubble, overgrazing, and intensive dryland farming methods are rarely perceived by anyone other than the knowledgeable wildlife biologist as a threat to bird populations. Meanwhile, the poor beleaguered gun-toting hunter is considered to be the prime enemy of wildlife.

I had made better than a dozen phone calls toward the end of the summer, trying to line up hunting access for opening day. I'd talked to game officers and landowners and had finally scored

permission from a rancher who, though he owned a relatively small piece of property, said that he had some birds.

Now I pulled into the parking lot of a café outside town where I was to meet Mastro. He was already there, sitting in his truck, of which I had never been more envious. I parked beside him in the Escort.

Mike looked down at me as I pulled up. "Traded the Suburban in for something more economical, huh, Jim?" he said.

"That's very funny, Mike," I answered.

"It'll look great pulling the Airstream," he said.

"Ha . . . ha . . . ha."

By the time we had followed my directions to the ranch the sun was well up. Now it was really getting hot.

"It's too damn hot for opening day," I said.

"We'll have to watch out for the dogs in this heat," Mastro answered.

We knocked on the door of the ranch house. The rancher himself answered. He was very accommodating and pointed up behind the house. "Just hunt up that draw," he said. "You'll find birds there. They like to be near water."

As we were talking to the rancher, a tiny, wizened old woman came out of another small house in the ranch compound and glared at us suspiciously. "Don't say anything to Mother about hunting her birds," the rancher added. "She's kind of protective of them."

"What shall we say we're doing?" I asked. "In case she asks."

"Don't say anything," he said. "Just pretend you're hunting deer. She doesn't mind that."

"Hunting deer with dogs and shotguns?"

"Don't worry; she won't know the difference."

So we drove down a two-track lane behind the ranch yard, parked, unloaded the dogs, and walked to the end of the draw— a small drainage that ran out of the hills to irrigate a meadow below. Although only an hour's drive from the wide open spaces

of the high mountain "park" in which I live, this country is on the other side of the Continental Divide in western Colorado and represents a different ecosystem altogether. Hardly mountains any longer, the hills hereabout seem as close-set as the hills of West Virginia and are covered mainly with scrub oak, cedar, and juniper.

At a couple of thousand feet of elevation lower, it was also considerably warmer than my home country. Still, Mike and I had been encouraged by the rancher's certainty of finding birds in the draw. Who knows? Maybe we'd get into them right away and be finished before the real heat of day set in. The daily bag limit on mountain sharptails is only two birds—down from twenty in the year 1915.

We worked up either side of the draw as the dogs quartered through the grass and shrubs in the bottom. Although neither of us had ever hunted them before, we'd been boning up the birds' habits and habitat by reading various Division of Wildlife publications and by talking to wildlife officers. Too, there is a universal element to all good game bird habitat, the basic requirements of which are really very simple—food, cover, and water—and hunters eventually develop a kind of sixth sense about where birds are likely to be found, even in unfamiliar country.

Now Mastro and I both remarked on how "birdy" the country looked (as in "well, it sure *looks* birdy")—which shows how much we knew, for as we worked up the draw from the meadow into the lightly timbered hills we found no sharptails, nor did any of the dogs act even remotely interested. We hit the rancher's fence line, grateful for the shade of the trees on the hill.

"I guess we'd better go back down to the house and ask him where his second-best spot is," Mike suggested.

This time the rancher sent us over to his alfalfa and wheat fields. "You'll find birds there, for sure," he assured us. His tiny old mother was still watching us from her doorway. She kind of gave me the creeps. It was getting hotter by the minute.

The country here was divided into a lot of small parcels, and the rancher's wheat and alfalfa fields were not contiguous to the rest of his property. It required a short drive and a couple of turn-offs, but we found the place, or so we believed.

We started working around the edge of the wheat field and through a likely-looking patch of mixed brush cover. We stopped frequently to rest and water the dogs. It was getting dangerously hot. In my journal entry of that day's hunt I have written: "I can't *ever* remember having hunted in such hot weather."

Then from the thick brush we heard a yelp from Mastro's young spaniel, Misty, who plowed, squealing, out of the cover with a face full of porcupine quills, at which exact moment a pickup truck came careening and bouncing down the two-track road toward us. Even before we could see the driver's face, we knew from the way he was driving that he was not coming to welcome us. It occurred to us both in the same instant and with an awful clarity that we must have taken a wrong turn and were inadvertently trespassing on someone else's land. "Uh-oh," I said as Mastro tried to calm his quill-stricken dog. "I think we have a problem here."

The truck pulled up short, and the driver, a small, wiry fellow, jumped from the cab and strode purposefully toward us. "You'd better get out of here!" said the man, his face flushed with anger. "You'd better get out off my property!" he added, waving his finger at us.

Menaced by the man's aggressive approach and obviously unaware that we were the trespassers, Sweetz started howling at him.

"Knock it off, Sweetz!" I hollered at her. "Sir, I'm sorry," I said to him. "Jack Soper [not his real name] gave us permission to hunt here." Even before the words were out of my mouth, I knew that this was not what I had meant to say.

And it made the little rancher even madder. "Jack Soper? Jack Soper gave you permission? Jack Soper *did not* give you

permission to hunt here!" he hollered, his face going scarlet with rage. Clearly this fellow had a heart attack in his future; I just hoped we weren't going to be the cause of it.

"I guess we got a little confused," I said lamely.

"You'd better get out of here," the rancher repeated. *"You'd better get the hell off my land! And tell your goddamn dog to stop barking at me or I'll shoot the miserable sonofabitch."*

"We're gone," I said. "We're outta here. Shut up, Sweetzer!"

As many bird hunters have found out the hard way, nothing puts a damper on a hunt more thoroughly than getting hollered at by a landowner for trespassing. It's a terrible way to start the season. Of course, it was entirely our own fault, though as Mike had pointed out, it would make things a whole lot easier for all concerned if property owners would simply post their land, especially in country as chopped up as this.

Although things were going rapidly from bad to worse, Mike and I still weren't prepared to give up on opening day just yet. Back at the truck we regrouped, pulled quills out of Misty's face, and decided to give it one last shot. The first thing we did was go back to the ranch house and get our directions straight. By now it must have been ninety-five degrees in the shade, easy.

This time the rancher was gone and a young woman answered the door. She looked too young to be the rancher's wife, too old to be his daughter. Later Mike and I both decided that she must be the rancher's live-in girlfriend. She introduced herself as Susie, and I recalled that I had spoken to her a couple of times on the phone over the summer while trying to arrange hunting permission. Now we exchanged pleasantries at the door. Susie was smoking a cigarette in a certain world-weary manner. She looked like she'd been around some.

"You come from this country, Susie?" I asked her, more by way of gauging the reliability of her information regarding resident bird populations than out of mere curiosity. Susie shook her head. "I come from all over—Utah, Nevada, Wyoming. My people are oil field trash."

Right off I liked Susie.

"Now what can I do for you boys?" she asked, taking a long, squinty pull on her cigarette. Then she kind of flicked her head back and expertly blew the smoke skyward so that it didn't go directly in our face through the screen door. "Tell me this: what's your goal?"

"Our goal?" I asked. This struck me as an odd question, though it did kind of fit with the slightly off-kilter nature of opening day so far. "Our goal is really very simple, Susie," I said. "Our goal is to shoot a couple of sharptail grouse. Or maybe just to see a couple. We just got busted by one of your neighbors for accidentally trespassing and we want to be sure not to make the same mistake again. He was not a bit happy to see us."

"Little terrierlike guy?" Susie asked. "Looks like he's going to grab your pant leg in his teeth and shake hell out of your leg?"

I nodded. "That's the one."

Susie waved her cigarette dismissingly. "That's Schroeder," she said. "Don't worry about him. Schroeder's never happy. He's pissed off at the whole world.

"Now if you're looking for birds," Susie continued, smoking reflectively, "I'd probably send you up to hunt the hillside above the stock tank. I've been seeing birds there all summer. Sometimes they're right down by the water. If you want, I'll take you up there myself. You can follow me in your truck."

Because hunters are eternal optimists, we allowed our spirits to rise slightly as we followed Susie, who drove one of the ranch trucks. She seemed quite competent and so certain about finding birds by the stock tank. But just as we were pulling out of the drive I noticed that the old woman was watching us again from her doorway.

"I think that old woman is jinxing our hunt," I said to Mike. "I got a weird feeling about it."

"Don't be ridiculous," Mike said.

"I'm serious," I said. "She gives me the creeps. I think she's

put a hex on us. She doesn't want us to find her birds, and that's why we've having such bad luck so far."

Mike hummed the *Twilight Zone* theme song: "*Do-do do-do, do-do do-do.*" "Maybe she even caused your truck to blow up yesterday, Jim," he remarked. "*Do-do do-do, do-do do-do.*"

Susie led us to the stock tank, showed us the hillside that we should hunt, and wished us luck. Now the midday heat was at its peak. I'll bet it was pushing a hundred degrees.

The hill was steep, covered with patches of scrub oak, mountain blackberry, chokecherry, and serviceberry. Not only was it hot, but it had been dry as well, the fruit on the berry bushes sparse and shriveled. The hillside had a certain tindery feel to it, as if at any moment it might burst spontaneously into flame. However, there was some shade and good cover and if I were a grouse, this was where I would loaf during the relentless midday heat.

We humped the whole length of the hillside—hard, hot work, climbing and busting brush—and did not come across a single bird. Rather than risk having a dog fall victim to heat prostration, which would turn a merely lousy opening day into a truly disastrous one, we decided to quit. We'd had enough. We were whipped.

"I don't know about you, but I've had better opening days," Mike observed as he drove me back to my rental car in Steamboat Springs.

"No kidding," I said. "Yesterday my truck blew up and all I could rent in Denver was a Ford Escort, which should have been my first tip-off that opening day was going to be a bust. Right off it was too damn hot to hunt; then your dog got into the porcupine and we got our asses chewed for trespassing. Now it's what? about ninety-eight degrees in the shade and we never even saw a bird. I think it's safe to say that we've both had better opening days."

"Well, at least no dogs died," Mastro pointed out.

We parted company in the parking lot of the café, promising to try another time for this species, maybe next season, as this year we were both headed in different directions.

But evidently the opening day hex wasn't off me just yet. On my way home I stopped at the grocery store in Steamboat Springs. As I pushed my cart past the meat counter, three college-age kids, a young man and two young women, presumably visiting one or another of their parents' condo (probably built in what was once prime mountain sharptail habitat) for the Labor Day weekend, were involved in an intense discussion over a package of chicken breasts, which the young man held in his hand. "*Totally* gross!" said one of the young women. "I can't eat that kind. Get the kind that doesn't have bones or skin on it." It occurred to me with a start that this person might actually believe that boneless, skinless chicken breasts were a separate subspecies of the gross kind with the bones and skins—kind of like the difference between mountain and plains sharptails in her urban mind.

"Yes, but what I'm trying to tell you is that I can take the skin and bones off," said the young man. "It's less expensive to buy it like this." There was hope yet for this lad.

"*Hello?* You're not listening to me," the young woman insisted. "It makes me sick even to look at the *bones!* I can't eat that *kind.* That kind is totally *gross!*"

I stepped up to the counter. Of course, I had not intended to call attention to myself, which is something hunters have learned to avoid at all cost these days—especially in cities and ski resorts. I thought I was pretty inconspicuous; needless to say, I was not carrying a shotgun in the supermarket, and I had taken off my orange hunting vest. I was, however, still wearing my old brush pants with bloodstains on them from past seasons, and I had forgotten to remove my whistle lanyard.

When I stepped up to the counter, the young man noticed me. "Say, you must be a bird hunter?" he asked very politely.

"Why, yes, I am; how'd you know that?" I asked. "Do you hunt?"

"My Uncle George lives in Kansas and I go every year to hunt quail with him on opening weekend," he said. "What kind of birds do they have around here?"

I told him. All the while the two young women were eyeing me with something between revulsion, hatred, and fear—as if I might suddenly whip out an automatic weapon and spray the place with gunfire.

Finally, the one who had the aversion to chicken bones spoke up. "You kill birds?" she asked her boyfriend in a tone of shocked disbelief, as if she had just learned some dark, relationship-busting secret about the young man. "That is so totally weird. *Hello?* I suppose you haven't heard that birds are going extinct at an unprecedented rate?" She was presumably quoting this last interesting factoid from the environmental literature she received in the mail.

On another day and in other circumstances, I might have tried to defend myself, and this young man, against such misrepresentation. I might have pointed out that it was hunters—such visionaries as George Bird Grinnell and Theodore Roosevelt—who had started the modern American conservation movement; that hunting license fees had funded the National Wildlife Refuge program and thousands of other habitat preservation and restoration efforts across the country; that such hunters' groups as Ducks Unlimited, Pheasants Forever, the Ruffed Grouse Society, and the Rocky Mountain Elk Foundation had created and protected more wildlife habitat, and hence more wildlife, than all the animal rights groups in the country combined. But I did not point these things out; sometimes you just have to admit that you're licked, that not only aren't you going to kill a game bird, but even a package of pick-of-the-chick is out of reach on opening day.

"Run for your life, kid," I warned the young man. "Get back to your Uncle George's as soon as you can."

And I fled myself, a fugitive from popular culture. As I made my escape from the resort grocery store, I flashed on the image of the little old ranch woman standing in her darkened doorway, beaming out bad fortune like a radio signal to those who would slay her birds. *Do-do do-do, do-do do-do* . . .

2

OPENING DAY II

It's déjà vu all over again.

—Yogi Berra

It's a funny thing, isn't it, how every hunt takes on its own specific atmosphere? Even the same hunt with the same companions in the same place will have a totally different feel year after year. This, of course, is the reason we keep coming back for more.

Another year had slipped away, and along about August I got to thinking about my hunting companion Mike Mastro. Mike and I had met at the Holland & Holland shooting school a couple of summers earlier. I was taking the school as part of a magazine assignment, and Mastro was also a student. As we were both from Colorado and had common interests in bird hunting and double shotguns, we had kept in touch. Although we did not see or talk to each other most of the year, come August, as in some kind of migrational memory reflex of hunters, one of us

would pick up the phone and call the other. First we'd catch up a little on the past year in our respective lives.

"You get a job yet, Mastro?" I asked Mike, who answered that he had managed to stay unemployed for almost the entire bird season last year and then went to travel agent school and had opened his own agency, which he hoped to tailor to the needs of traveling sportsmen. Of course, being involved in a similar scam as an outdoor writer, I immediately saw through Mastro's transparency. "Sure, that way maybe you'll get comped by the lodges and outfitters when you research destinations for your clients. And of course, all your sport will be tax-deductible as a business expense."

"Exactly," Mike said.

Eventually, the conversation worked its way around to the subject of opening day. "You ever get back to hunt those mountain sharptail last year?" Mike asked.

"Never did," I answered. "I was thinking that maybe we should try it again this year."

"I'm available," Mike said.

This time opening day dawned a fine cool September morning, a true fall day, hunting weather for sure. Sweetz and I loaded up in the Suburban; yes, the Suburban (knock on wood) was running, if not exactly like a Swiss clock, then at least pretty well for a ten-year-old vehicle with 200,000 miles on it. As we were driving out the dirt cutoff road that would take us over to Steamboat Springs, we passed another bird hunter who was heading from the other direction into my country to hunt sage grouse. He was behind the wheel of an old International Scout, and the reason I knew he was a bird hunter was because he wore a hunting vest and had an English setter in the tiny front seat with him. The setter, presumably all excited about opening day, was trying to lick its master on the face, and as our vehicles

passed the man was laughing and trying to pull his head away from his dog's lashing tongue. It was just a momentary encounter, just two hunters passing on a gravel road at dawn on opening day, but the scene put me in an even better mood.

Mike and I met at the same hour on the same day in the same parking lot of the same café outside Steamboat Springs. And I had arranged to hunt the same rancher's property again. Access is so limited in this country that you take what you can get and are grateful for it, too. But I had a good feeling about this year.

The rancher was still in bed when we arrived and finally answered our knocks dressed only in his jockey shorts. I have noticed this about ranchers and farmers: often they answer the door wearing only their underpants, or even less. I have no idea why. Perhaps they're trying to scare us off. Recently when I stopped to ask permission to hunt quail on a farm in Kansas, the farmer, whom I must have just woken from his afternoon nap, answered the door dressed only in a shirt and no underpants at all. And he was—I don't know how to say this politely—aroused. And didn't seem in the least bit self-conscious about it, either.

Now I peered past the rancher and noticed that his living room was a real mess, much more so than last year; it had the look of a bachelor's house, and it occurred to me that Susie must have moved on. I was sorry about that; I had really liked old Susie.

The rancher scratched his chest sleepily and told us that we should try hunting around his wheat and alfalfa fields—to which this time we got really specific directions. I even drew a little map in my notebook just to be safe and made some joke about hoping not to run into Schroeder this year. "Oh, I wouldn't worry too much about that," the rancher said. "Schroeder dropped dead of a heart attack while he was feeding his cows last winter."

"I knew it," I said to Mastro as we walked back to the truck. "We killed Schroeder." Now I looked over at the little cottage,

but there was no sign of the rancher's tiny, wizened mother—which I took to be another good sign.

This time we drove right to the fields—no problem; last year we'd been on the wrong side of the road is all. And this year Schroeder's property was posted about every thirty yards with brand-new, not-to-be-misunderstood NO HUNTING/NO TRESPASSING signs, just as Mike had suggested. Too late for Schroeder, of course.

We parked the truck, unloaded the dogs, unsheathed guns, and headed for the corner between the wheat field and the alfalfa field. A covey of sharptails got up, and I connected on the first shot of the season—another good omen. Then Mike killed a brace and I whiffed on an easy going-away shot (just so that the day wouldn't be too perfect) and less than an hour into the opener we decided to call it quits. I was quite satisfied with my one bird. As Susie would have said, that had been my "goal" from the beginning, and I had achieved it.

We stopped at the ranch house on the way out to thank our host, but he was nowhere to be found. As we were walking around looking for him, the little old woman, more wizened than ever, came out of her cottage and squinted hard at us.

"Damn," I muttered under my breath, "almost a clean getaway."

"You fellas get any deer this morning?" she hollered.

"No, ma'am," we both answered happily in unison.

"We sure didn't," Mike said, shaking his head regretfully.

"We didn't even see any deer, ma'am," I added for good measure.

3

THE AIR UP THERE

The prairie falcon was the principal avian predator and the red
fox was the principal carnivore responsible for ptarmigan
mortality. In Rocky Mountain National Park, traffic on the
heavily used highway bisecting the study units caused some
mortality. One chick died in the park when a tourist
inadvertently stepped on it. Occasionally tourists were observed
trying to stone ptarmigan on the study areas, but no mortality
from stoning was documented.

> *The White-tailed Ptarmigan in Colorado*
> —Clait E. Braun and Glenn E. Rogers,
> State of Colorado—Division of Game, Fish and Parks
> Technical Publication Number Twenty-seven

I admit that Sweetz and I started out on a kind of quest that
season. And I don't think it was necessarily a good thing, either.
I think possibly it obscured the true purpose of bird hunting . . .
at least to me, for Sweetz spends considerably less time than I
brooding over such matters, which only goes to prove that a

dog's interest in sport is utterly pure—a simple, monklike de-votion to the Bird God.

For my part, I had figured out over the summer that there were only four game bird species resident to the continental United States that Sweetz had not retrieved in her career, and oddly, for all our traveling around the country during hunting season, two of them, including the white-tailed ptarmigan, lived within an hour's drive from home (albeit a three-hour hike straight up the mountain after that). Having covered the moun-tain sharptail on the western side of the Continental Divide, we now set off for a climbing expedition on the eastern side.

I had been studying up during the summer on the white-tailed ptarmigan (*Lagopus leucurus*), an extraordinary little bird. The smallest member of the grouse family, it lives out its extraordi-nary life at a twelve-thousand-plus-foot elevation. No other game bird on earth occupies a harsher ecosytem—ranging from its summer habitat in the alpine tundra above tree line to the subalpine basins where it winters. The white-tailed ptarmigan is also unique (except for *Lagopus lagopus scoticus*) in that it changes from a mottled gray-and-brown plumage that perfectly mimics the summer tundra terrain, making it nearly indistin-guishable from a lichen-covered rock, to a pure snow-white in winter that makes it a dead-ringer for a snowball.

But even the rarefied and inaccessible range of the white-tailed ptarmigan has not made it safe from the invasive activities of man. Besides the threat from the aforementioned *tourii* in Rocky Mountain National Park, the relentless encroachment of the ski industry, the building of water storage reservoirs in sub-alpine drainages, and high-altitude mining activities have all exacted a toll on ptarmigan populations and traditional range in Colorado. In addition to these pressures, overgrazing by both domestic cattle and wild ungulates continues to alter ptarmigan habitat. This latter poses a particular problem in Rocky Moun-tain National Park, where a severely overpopulated elk herd (al-though park managers are loath to admit it) is overrunning the

ptarmigan's winter and summer ranges, threatening in the process, (without some form of controlled hunting and/or the introduction of wolves) to turn the place into a Disneyesque Elk Theme Park.

As is so often the case, the hunter is nearly as insignificant a cause of ptarmigan mortality as the occasional heavy-footed or rock-wielding tourist. Although you can drive to the bird's habitat in Rocky Mountain National Park, you of course can't hunt them there. Pretty much everywhere else you have to hike to it—uphill, in progressively thinner air—and even then the birds can be extremely difficult to locate. In this way, ptarmigan hunting is a kind of "extreme" sport, which tends to be self-limiting. For exactly the same reason, the ptarmigan tends to have far fewer natural predators than other grouse species. Like the human hunter, it is the rare fox or coyote who will go to all the trouble and expenditure of energy to hike up to ptarmigan country for what will, in the best of circumstances, be a dicey shot at a meal. Even avian predators such as hawks and eagles can usually locate more easily taken prey. In fact, the adult white-tailed ptarmigan has the highest annual survival rate of any other grouse species. (Studies suggest as high as 71 percent, as opposed to 6–28 percent in comparable studies on ruffed grouse in Minnesota.) One bird banded by Colorado Division of Wildlife biologist Clait Braun, the country's foremost authority on the white-tailed ptarmigan, lived to the astonishing age of fifteen years—a longevity virtually unheard of in any other gallinaceous game bird on earth.

Early that morning, opening day of the ptarmigan season, I met a fellow named Jake Brinkman and his friend Rex at a Dairy Queen off the interstate. Brinkman, who hailed originally from East Kentucky, spoke with a laconic John Wayne–like drawl and sported a thick, dark mustache, a USMC tattoo on his arm, and a perpetual good-natured smile. Jake was a maintenance engi-

neer for the Boulder Valley School District, and his buddy Rex, a quiet, wiry fellow, was a courier for same. They were a couple of solid hard working blue-collar Americans.

A friend of a bird-hunting friend, Brinkman had agreed, after some negotiations, to take me to his ptarmigan "honeyhole," a spot that he had been hunting successfully for the past eight seasons. Ptarmigan tend to have a limited lateral range, summering and wintering year after year, generation after generation, in more or less the same places, and as long as hunters are careful not to take more than 20 percent of the covey in any given year, the populations will remain stable. Brinkman, who naturally thought of these birds as "his ptarmigan" (all bird hunters know the feeling, and most of us respect each other's proprietorship), had learned a great deal about the species and had conscientiously husbanded the covey over the years. As it was, he had only agreed to take me to his honeyhole under the standard terms of the bird's hunter contract: (1.) I would never return here alone or with anyone but him; (2.) I would never reveal to anyone else even the general location of "his birds"; and (3.) this was a one-time-only offer.

Agreed.

And so we drove to the trailhead and set out. It was a mild, perfect early fall day, but we each carried day packs with foul-weather gear and emergency camping supplies. As mountain climbers know—and sometimes tragically learn the hard way—the weather can change dramatically in a matter of minutes at such altitudes, and one must come prepared for the possibility of a mild sunny morning that feels like summer turning into an afternoon whiteout of dead winter.

We hiked first through mixed conifer aspen woods, as lush as a rain forest after the moist summer, with ferns and wild mushrooms and wildflowers in abundance. I made a mental note to pick some mushrooms on the way back down—they'd go well on the table with the ptarmigan.

We traversed the mountainside, steadily gaining altitude,

breaking out of the forest finally into a subalpine drainage and a series of beaver ponds that spilled down the draw to the valley below. As we climbed, the thick stands of fir gave way to smaller groupings of twisted, stunted trees and then to a last few hearty individuals struggling valiantly uphill. In the same way, the cinquefoil and willows grew progressively lower to the ground the higher we climbed, as if hunkering down out of the relentless wind that sweeps from the treeless peaks above. There seems something heroic about all things that have adapted to living at this altitude.

Higher still we entered the alpine tundra itself, oddly and briefly lush this time of year, the hillsides covered in short green grass speckled by intensely red Indian paintbrush, bluebells, and tiny, delicate dark green ferns, the latter a main staple of the ptarmigan's summer diet.

Now we stopped to rest more frequently, to take off our packs, lay down our guns, and drink some water. "Every year this hike gets a little tougher," Brinkman admitted. "But it's worth it just to be up here, isn't it?"

Yes, it was. The world looked particularly magnificent from this vantage point, above most of the other mountain peaks, with a view that went on forever.

"Look at the white butterfly sitting on that daisy," Brinkman said with wonder, bringing our gaze back into close focus. Strangely formed and brilliantly colored grasshoppers, the likes of which I had never before seen, squirted out around us. Rex, who had an interest in entomology, caught one and put it a film canister to take back as a specimen. Like the ptarmigan, there are creatures and plants that live up here and nowhere else. There is a sense on the tundra of being on another planet altogether, and I felt an incredible sense of good fortune to be able to get here under power of my own two legs, to see these wonders. . . . But perhaps my euphoria was partly a result of oxygen deprivation.

Oddly, the dogs didn't seem nearly as affected by the altitude as were we humans; I had been concerned about Sweetz's bad elbows, but I needn't have worried. She loped easily uphill without even breaking a hard pant, keeping pace with Brinkman's young shorthair, Max. Jake estimated that we had now reached 12,500 feet above sea level, at which altitude twenty paces begin to seem like the cardiovascular equivalent of a marathon.

We gained a steep, rocky hillside, and the edge of Brinkman's honeyhole. Below us a spring flowed through a basin to form a series of perfectly clear, shallow alpine pools. Ice formed around the edges of the water holes, and below that a perpetual snowfield glittered in the sun. According to Jake, the ptarmigan hang out in these rocks, so perfectly camouflaged that often you have to catch a glint from their small black eyes to spot them. Already I could imagine the little birds peeling up out of the rocks, like rocks themselves hurtling down the mountainside.

We noticed that between our mountain peak and the next over ominous storm clouds were forming. "We'll have to keep an eye on those," said Brinkman. "I've been up here when lightning was popping off the ground all around me. It's just amazing how fast you can get down off this mountain."

We worked across the bowl but failed to bump any birds. We broke for a rest and lunch. It occurred to me that the last time I ate lunch above 12,000 foot elevation it was served by a flight attendant on a plastic tray.

"I don't understand it," Jake said. "In eight years hunting here, I've never not run into birds by now. Maybe because it's been so mild this fall they're up higher still."

I'd heard the old ptarmigan-hunting adage that if you don't find the birds, go higher . . . so higher we went, 13,000 feet and climbing.

Now in the valley between the mountains, the storm clouds had in an instant massed and darkened and begun to roll and roil. Lightning flashed from within them, and a curtain of snow undulated toward us like a living, breathing entity—both beau-

tiful and ominous at once. In the face of such force and grandeur, my scheme to add this little bird to mine and Sweetz's life
list seemed suddenly ludicrous, meaningless—disrespectful to the
ptarmigan and blasphemous to the hunting gods. "Here it
comes!" Jake called up to me. "We'd better get down off this
mountain. Right now." I whistled Sweetz back in; she left her
scent trail reluctantly, kept trying to circle back to it. Somewhere just up ahead, just a little higher, a covey of those magnificent little birds was hunkered down in the rocks, waiting for
the intruders to leave, waiting for the first snows of winter to
cover the tundra, to keep pace with their already slightly mottled white-and-gray plumage, to complete the transition anew.
While we ran from the black clouds of the approaching storm,
which could mean death to us, the ptarmigan looked forward to
the whiteness that gave them life.

4

COCKTAILS WITH POOPS

To Joseph R. Walton
(July 2, 1931–December 12, 1997)
In memoriam

It was still early in the bird season, and I was sitting up at the bar of a local restaurant with my neighbor Joe Walton—or Poops, I call him, affectionately, because he's a bit of an old poop. We were having a martini before dinner.

Ordinarily we drove to the restaurant together, but this time I had arranged to meet Poops, who is not a hunter, at the restaurant, because Sweetz and I were going to stop off on the way at one of our "home coverts"—our own little secret sage grouse spot, which we hunted every year early in the season, usually successfully. Soon we would be leaving home again on our regular fall tour, and I always liked to hunt our home covey just once before we did so as a kind of talisman. There are certain rituals, traditions, and superstitions in this sporting life that must be rigidly adhered to, and this was one of them. My wife, as she

often does at the first hint of fall in the air, had already left home herself for warmer climes—also a kind of annual tradition.

"So how was the hunting?" Poops asked me, but without any genuine interest.

"I found my covey and just shot one first-year bird out of it," I said. "You want to come over for a sage grouse dinner this week?"

This was a little private joke between me and Poops, because one year I actually did have him over for sage grouse and he so hated the admittedly somewhat pungent wild bird that he never let me forget it. Poops is strictly a domestic-meat kind of guy.

The truth is Poops and I have almost nothing in common, except that we are both originally midwesterners and we both like martinis—which I guess is common ground enough, because we're very good friends in spite of our differences. This is one of the fine things about living, even part of the year as we both do, in a very small town—you get to know something of the lives of people with whom you would hardly cross paths in a city.

I tend to think of Poops, in his middle sixties now, although he looks a decade younger, as the last representative of the Eisenhower era—a fifties kind of guy, very conservative, a staunch believer in the general rightness of postwar America. I myself, twenty years younger, am a product of that next, disenfranchised generation—which, though running the show now, or trying to, is still filled with cynicism and anger and a different, though no less twisted, reality.

Poops is a portly, endomorphic fellow—a very deliberate, slow-moving sort—while I tend toward the ectomorphic: lean, frenetic, spewing type-A behavior like a vapor trail. Poops is a lifelong bachelor. His father, with whom he was not close, died when he was a young man, and after he got out of the army he came home and lived all of his adult life with his mother, who only recently died peacefully in her nineties—alert and active right to the end. Poops worked for thirty-five years for the same

insurance company where he moved up steadily through the middle-management ranks to eventually run the Phoenix branch office. He attended all of the company functions and conventions, made many lifelong friends among his coworkers, and was well liked and respected by all. He took early retirement with a generous package from the company (when such was still available) and with a nice little savings nest egg, for he and his mother were thrifty, hardworking middle-class Americans (when such still existed). As we are all of us products of our own eras, Poops exited the business world just in time, just on the cusp of the radical change brought about by the revolution in computer technology, spiraling growth, the health-care "crisis," and a new general spirit of incivility and no-holds-barred mean-spiritedness that shortly would have made him obsolete in the workplace anyway. In many ways, Poops has led a comfortable, well-managed, timely, I would go so far as to say, even charmed life, for it has also been a life relatively free of major heartbreak and disappointments.

Of course, I'm a married man myself and, as a writer, have never held much of anything in the way of a steady job. When I contemplate the retirement benefits of my own profession, I tend to think of a fleabag hotel, a pack of Camels, a bottle of scotch, and my last unpawned shotgun. Not that I'm complaining, mind you, for truly I have led a blessed life myself, and I only mention this by way of contrasting the deep differences in the respective realities of me and my old friend Poops.

Even our interest in nature and the outdoors is light-years apart, Poops's tending to be specific to what he can see out the window of his car and living room. One time over cocktails just after he had his lawn sprayed for weeds, I made some mention of an article in one of my bird publications about the fact that some of the chemicals used on lawns might be hazardous to songbirds.

"Oh, come on, Jim," scoffed Poops. "What's more important, people and green lawns or birds?"

Still, I find something enormously comforting, even enviable, about Poops's life, about his whole personality, outlook, and philosophy—his placid, unshakable faith in the general rightness of things.

So now Poops and I were sitting up at the bar having a predinner cocktail and sneaking a smoke. Well, Poops doesn't have to sneak; he's a lifelong smoker, and though he's tried to quit once or twice, he holds firm to the also seriously out-of-fashion belief that the dangers of smoking are vastly overstated by the media and medical establishments. However, Poops is not stupid, and he stops short of believing the tobacco company presidents—that unconscionable pack of liars who stood up a few years ago in front of Congress, raised their right hands, and solemnly swore to the American people that they did not believe nicotine was an addictive substance. No, Poops pretty much accepts the fact that he's a junkie like anyone else who fools with nicotine in any form. "You have to die of something," he says with a shrug.

"You want me to tell you more about my sage grouse hunt?" I asked now as we sipped our martinis and smoked our cigarettes. Because another of our private jokes is how truly uninterested Joe is in anything that has to do with hunting. "Not really," said Poops, and he made a mock sad face. "*Poor* little birds."

"Hey, Poops, remember how you had hurt feelings that you weren't mentioned in my hunting book?" I asked. "Well, it's on account of just such attitudes as that. You won't even listen to my stories."

"Well, you mentioned just about everyone in town except your old friend and neighbor," he said.

"Yeah, because you don't hunt," I said. "How can you expect me to mention you in a book about bird hunting if you don't even hunt? I mean what am I going to write about, 'Cocktails with Poops'?"

"Yes," he said firmly. "Why not?"

Now the bartender sidled over. She was a tall, handsome,

healthy-looking woman with dark hair and dark eyes, and I'd never seen her before in the area. "I thought I heard you mention something about bird hunting," she said. "I'm a bird hunter myself."

"Really?" I said. "Yes, I was hunting sage chickens before I came over here."

Now she leaned down on the bar and looked me right in the eye. "Find any birds?" she asked.

Uh-oh. Bird hunters have a sixth sense for this sort of thing. I already knew that the bartender was going to try to weasel out of me the location of my sage grouse honeyhole. But just then she got called by another patron down the bar. Whew! Saved by the bell.

"I think the new bartender likes you," Poops said.

"No, you don't understand," I said, "not being a hunter. What she likes is my secret sage grouse spot. I can see it in her eyes."

"Nooooo," Poops insisted, nodding and smiling slyly. "I don't think so. I think she likes you. And your wife is out of town. I wonder: what's my silence worth?"

"It's not worth a damn thing, you old poop," I said, "because there's nothing to be silent about. I'm a happily married man and you're a damn troublemaker."

Now the bartender came back over. She put both her hands on the bar and leaned over closer to me. It's true that she plain looked like trouble.

"I've never seen you around here before," I said.

"I've been wrangling horses all summer at the D Lazy U," she said. (The D Lazy U is a dude ranch in the next valley over from ours.) "The season just ended and I'm heading back up to Montana. I've got family here and stopped off to see them, figured I may as well work for a month. I like to visit my family in September, when I can hunt the blue grouse in the mountains." Now she looked hard at me with dark, penetrating eyes. My mouth went dry under the heat of her gaze. "I got some good blue grouse spots," she said. Yep, I knew it was coming.

"Excuse me just a moment," she added, pulling away to serve a couple who had just entered.

Now Poops was really chortling. "What's it going to cost?" he said. "*What's* it going to cost?"

"What are you talking about?" I said still flushed. "I haven't done a damn thing. Why do I need to buy your silence? This is a matter between bird hunters. Can't you see that? A very delicate process of negotiation."

"Oh, right, bird hunters!" Poops said, shaking his head. "James, James, James," he chortled. "Even if that were true," he added, "you'll never have a future as a professional negotiator."

"Oh, yeah? Well you watch me. She's going to come back here and try to find out the location of my sage grouse honeyhole. Then we'll just see how I do in the negotiation department."

Straightaway the bartender came back, leaned down again, fixed me with her eyes. "What's your name anyway?"

"Jim," I said, "and this is Joe. What's yours?"

"Crystal," she answered standing straight. She stuck her hand out forthrightly. She had a large hand with strong fingers befitting a wrangler, an iron grip. "Pleased to meet you fellas."

"So, Jim," Crystal continued, "back to this bird-hunting business. How'd you like to take me out after sage grouse sometime?"

"Gee, I don't know, Crystal," I said. "You know, I've got a couple of general spots . . . but I don't usually take anyone there. Especially locals who might be tempted to go back without me. Being a bird hunter yourself, you know how it is."

Crystal nodded thoughtfully, seemed to consider this. She took a deep breath and kind of stretched like a cat, arching her back, which effect strained the snap buttons on the front of her western-style shirt. Like I say, she was a large, healthy woman, and . . . well . . . it was the sort of gesture that was more or less impossible not to notice. "Oh, sure," she said. "I understand."

Now Crystal leaned down again, her large hands spread on the bar top, like a cat poised to jump. "I tell you what, Jim,"

she said in a low voice. She looked around as if to see if anyone was listening in, but it was just me and Poops. "You take me out in the flats and show me your sage chicken," she continued locking her eyes on mine like a heat-seeking missile. "and I'll take you up into the timber and show you my blue grouse . . . that's my offer. Now you think about that." Then she pushed off from the bar with both hands and went back to work without another glance our way.

"Crystal," I muttered sweatily to Poops. "Wouldn't you just know her name would be Crystal?"

Poops took a long contemplative drag on his cigarette; he uses one of those tar-trapping plastic filters, which makes him look something like a cross between the forties movie actors Sidney Greenstreet and Peter Lorre. "You know, I think if I was a bird hunter," he said on the exhale, "I might just want to take a peek at Crystal's blue grouse."

And that's how my friend and neighbor Joe Walton, aka Poops, finally got his name in a story about bird hunting.

5

FROM SWEETZER TO MIKE

I was talking on the phone one day to my accountant, a fellow named Mike Benninghoven. Although Mike was a numbers guy and I am a word guy, we had gotten to know each other over the phone in the course of several years and had discovered a mutual interest in fishing and bird hunting—the great common denominators.

Mike knew of a secret trout lake high in the mountains near where I live, and he liked to take his kids up there camping and fishing. The lake had big fish in it, he told me, and no one else seemed to know about it. He was a generous man, Mike, and earlier that summer had actually told me the name of the lake, its location, even how to get there. Although I hadn't gone yet, I could scarcely believe that Mike would divulge such precious information to me, and I liked him all the more for that.

Now, with bird season open, Benninghoven casually mentioned that while deer and elk hunting over the past several seasons he'd come across a great blue grouse covert in the moun-

tains near where I live and would I like to go up there with him and try it next weekend?

Although in the state of Colorado populations of blue grouse (d. *Dendragapus obscurus*), of which there are eight distinct subspecies across the western United States, are generally stable and healthy, a recent five-year banding study by the Colorado Division of Wildlife showed less than 5 percent return of bands by hunters—suggesting a general lack of enthusiasm for the species among bird hunters. It's partly that because the blue grouse's natural habitat is in the mountains hunting them can be very hard work, involving a good deal of climbing, and, like ptarmigan, these birds themselves are difficult to locate. (Yet as with most species, a covert is a covert and if left intact and not overshot will usually produce birds year after year.) Furthermore, due to their habit of feeding as unwarily as domestic chickens on the forest floor or sitting passively on tree branches to peer down upon the hunter with simple, trusting bird curiosity, many hunters do not consider blue grouse to offer particularly "sporting" shooting. They are, however, a fine game bird on the table—especially early in the season, when their diet consists largely of various fall berries. And in order that the hunter does not have to put himself in the unpleasant position of contemplating the ethical violation that a bird in a tree might raise, a flushing dog can come in mighty handy. Blue grouse are much more likely to fly vigorously when kicked up by a dog—surely a genetically learned response from millennia of experience with foxes, coyotes, and wolves as predators.

So when Benninghoven invited me to go blue grouse hunting, to take me to his honeyhole, I said, "Sure. And I'll bring the dog," because Mike didn't have a bird dog.

"You mean I'll get to hunt with the famous Sweetzer?" Mike asked.

"Yeah, but don't get too excited about it," I said. "She's just another half-trained bird dog."

Well, it's not Sweetz's fault (it so rarely is), but it's true that

over the past few years, busy with this and that, I had let her do some serious backsliding in the performance of her bird dog duties. My friend Guy says that everyone screws up their first Lab, and while I didn't make a complete mess of things, it's also quite true that early on I made some basic beginner trainer mistakes—things that have dogged us (bad pun!) all of Sweetz's career. I managed to fix one or two of these training shortcomings, but not all of them. For instance, I've more or less gotten her to stop jumping in front of pointing dogs to flush the birds they're holding (a major relief to those of my friends who own pointers, I can tell you), but I never have gotten her steady to flush or shot.

The appointed day arrived and Mike met me at my cabin. Together we drove up into the mountains—on a rough dirt two-track up over a high pass at timberline, down the switchbacks on the other side to a small creek bottom, across the creek, up another dirt road, and down another, until the road dead-ended and Mike announced: "This is the spot." I already knew from our many phone conversations during the past few tax seasons that Mike was a competent sportsman, with an excellent sense of direction—an ability that I think may somehow be connected with a facility for numbers but, in my case at least, clearly not with language. I have tried, for instance, to talk myself out of being lost on numerous occasions, and it almost never works, whereas if you have the ability to sit down and do some simple figuring you're often back in business.

Now we worked our way up the mountainside on a faint game trail that roughly followed along a small spring and was overgrown with snowberry, wild raspberry, and rose hips. The trees on the slopes were mixed aspen, lodgepole pine, and fir. It was a good, strenuous hike but not a backbreaker, and the day was beautiful—cool, with the leaves on the aspen just beginning to turn. In no time at all we were into the birds, and we spread out across the slopes and enjoyed some fine shooting. Mike's blue grouse covert was a beauty, that was for sure.

It was growing late and we had nearly filled our respective limits and were preparing to head back down to our vehicle, parked at the trailhead. Mike I were walking down the trail when Sweetz put up a blue grouse in front of us. It flew across the trail heading downhill on Mike's side; he swung and shot, but the bird set its wings and sailed off unscathed. "Damn, that bird was *really* moving," Mike said. "I couldn't get in front of it."

Sweetz had taken off down the mountain in pursuit of the bird, one of her most annoying habits, though one that has been tempered now by age. I whistled at her, but she ignored me, then I hollered and whistled some more, but she just kept on hauling ass downhill through the forest, chasing the bird until she disappeared from sight.

"There, you see," I said somewhat sheepishly to Mike, "the famous gundog in action. She'll probably be back down at the truck by the time she stops chasing that bird." And so we broke open our guns and headed back down the trail ourselves.

After ten minutes had passed and Sweetz had still failed to return, I began to worry a bit about the possibility of her being lost in the woods. She might have chased that grouse to the next valley over for all I knew. So we stopped, and I whistled again, and finally we heard the sound of her breaking brush beneath us, and suddenly Sweetz appeared out of the undergrowth with Mike's grouse in her mouth.

She brought the bird to me, and upon examination we found that it had a single spot of blood on its head where a single pellet of #7 ½ shot had entered. Sometimes head-shot birds will set their wings and fly for a hundred yards or more before dropping stone dead from the air. "Well, I guess you didn't miss that bird after all," I said to Mike, handing the grouse to him. In her bird dog wisdom Sweetz must have sensed that bird had been hit all along and had decided that in this case slavish obedience to her master was less important than making the retrieve.

"I never saw a feather come off that bird," Mike said, marveling. "I'd have sworn I made a clean miss. What a great retrieve! That's a bird we never would have recovered without her. Thank you, Sweetz," he said, getting down to fawn over her. "What a great dog you've got, Jim!"

"It's all in the training, Mike," I answered.

It was the end of a perfect day, a perfect hunt, and we walked back down the trail to the vehicle, both of us with game pouches heavy. Mike just couldn't stopped bragging on his new best friend, Sweetz.

Epilogue

That was the first and the last time I ever hunted with Mike Benninghoven. The following summer, he had a seizure in Kennedy Airport in New York, and shortly thereafter he was diagnosed with an inoperable brain tumor. Mike kept working as long as he was able. He could still crunch the numbers in his head, but gradually the tumor began to affect his ability to speak. He still thought clearly, but the words came out all wrong and, eventually, not at all. We spoke a number of times on the phone when he was still able to do so. No matter how painful it was for him to find the words, he always asked about Sweetz, always made mention of that last retrieve.

I haven't been back to Mike's grouse covert since. Every year along about September I think about going back up there; I always intend to go. I remember the place perfectly, know just how to get there and where to find the birds, and maybe one day I will go back. I know Mike wouldn't mind—in fact, he would want me to have his grouse covert, because he was a generous man. But I just haven't been able to bring myself to go up there. In my mind's eye, I still hold the image of that last blue grouse of the day, the last grouse of Mike's life as it hap-

pened, sailing out across the trail in front of us, Mike swinging on it, and Sweetzer setting off down the mountain in hot pursuit. It's an image locked in memory and time, and I'm afraid if I go back I'll only spoil it.

6

UNDERCOVER ASSIGNMENT
IN DESOLATION CANYON

*The canyon is very tortuous, the river very rapid, and many lateral
canyons enter on either side. These usually have their branches so
that the region is cut into a wilderness of gray and brown cliffs . . .
crags and tower-shaped peaks are seen everywhere, and away
above them, long lines of broken cliffs, and above and beyond the
cliffs are pine forests, of which we obtain occasional glimpses as we
look up through a vista of rocks. The walls are almost without
vegetation; a few dwarf bushes are seen here and there, clinging to
the rocks, and cedars grow from the crevices—not like the cedars of
a land refreshed with rains, great cones bedecked with spray but
ugly clumps, like war clubs beset with spines. We are minded to
call this the Canyon of Desolation.*
—John Wesley Powell,
    The Exploration of the Colorado River and Its Canyons

It was to be a three-day chukar hunt/white-water raft trip
through Desolation and Gray Canyons on the Green River in

Utah—a somewhat complicated trip, as the outfitters had to put in upriver two days earlier and float down to meet us, while we hunters and our dogs were flying in by chartered plane to a remote private airstrip. My bird-hunting friend Mike Mastro had organized the adventure, but in midsummer both he and his friend had to drop out and so I had picked up the ball. I had to scramble to fill the vacancies and finally lined up a couple of the usual suspects—the painter Len Chmiel and photographer Steve Collector. Everything was set: dates scheduled with outfitters, backcountry pilot reserved, deposits made, days on the calendar marked off . . . well, almost everything. The only thing lacking for me and Collector was a hard assignment from a magazine, but I knew this is to be a mere formality and sent off my query with perfect confidence; even the most myopic New York magazine editor would recognize this as a great adventure story.

"Not interested?" I said incredulously to my editor on the phone when he finally got back to me a mere two weeks before Steve, Len, and I were scheduled to depart. "What do you mean, not interested? This is a great story. Wild canyon country, white-water rafting, chukar hunting, maybe even some fishing in the side canyons. How could you possibly not be interested in this story?"

"I'm afraid it just doesn't float my boat," he said.

"Doesn't float your boat?" I repeated in disbelief. *"Doesn't float your boat?"* It's true that magazine editors need to get out of New York more often. "But I've already set everything up."

Hunting trips, like military campaigns, have a way of taking on a life of their own, and once the often-lengthy process of organization is under way it can be next to impossible to abort them. In my mind the trip had been set in motion. Sure, maybe it didn't float my editor's boat, but my boats may as well have already been launched, the plane aloft, and I'd be damned if I was going to let it fall apart now.

"I thought it was a firm assignment," said Collector, who

tends to be more practical than I. (As the father of two young sons, he rather has to be.) "Look; if we don't have a paying gig, I'm out." It goes without saying that we writers and photographers are a threadbare bunch who are hardly in a position to hire outfitters on exotic trips for recreational purposes.

"We'll do it on spec," I argued. "Trust me. It's a great story. Somebody'll buy it."

"Forget it, Jim," said Collector. Steve and I have been knocking around in the magazine business together for going on twenty years now, and we've both learned the hard way never to do anything on spec. "But I might be able to sell it to *Sports Afield*," he added.

"I'm not allowed to work for *Sports Afield*," I said. "You know that."

Well, it was just the sort of preposterous, exploitative arrangement that only freelance writers or their close working man kin, Chilean mine laborers, would ever submit to. Even though we "field editors" were neither official employees of the company, and thus not eligible for benefits, nor paid enough by them to make our sole living, we were still forbidden to write for other like publications.

"Maybe you could write the story for *Sports Afield* under a pen name," Collector suggested.

"A pen name?" I said.

"Sure. Why not?" Steve said. "We still have two weeks. Start growing a beard right now, buy a different hat, and go on the trip incognito. Who'll be the wiser?"

"An undercover assignment for the competition?" I mused. "A double agent . . . I like it. Of course, you'd have to keep me out of the photographs."

"No problem. I'll only shoot you from behind," Steve assured me.

"What about Sweetz?" I asked. "Someone might recognize her in the photos."

"Jim," Steve said patiently, "I don't think anyone will be able to tell Sweetz from any other yellow Lab."

"Yeah, I guess I'm being a little paranoid," I admitted.

Now, two weeks later, we were aloft in a chartered Cessna 206 above the little town of Green River, Utah—three passengers, four dogs, and sundry gear. We flew high above the river, over the magnificent canyon country through which we would be floating for the next several days.

The largest tributary of the Colorado River, the Green River headwaters in the Wind River Mountains of Wyoming, flows south into the Uinta Mountains at the Wyoming-Utah border and hooks briefly east into Colorado before turning west and south again, back into Utah. John Wesley Powell ran the river in 1869 and again in 1871–72, the first leg of his historic explorations of the Colorado River. Powell didn't seem to care much for the country, seemed intimidated and clearly depressed by its harshness, aridity, and general inhospitality, and he referred to this stretch of the Green as a "region of the wildest desolation" and named the canyons we would be floating through Desolation and Gray Canyons, respectively.

Powell's distaste for the country may have had something to do with the fact that his trip wasn't exactly recreational, either. Nor was he a chukar hunter. Indeed, it would be more than a half-century before chukars were even introduced to the region. Which was too bad for Powell and his men, for in a real sense these wonderful little game birds seem to round out and complete the country—it's as if Nature meant to put them here but just forgot. And to the bird hunter no country with game birds can ever be called desolate.

Now just as we were becoming accustomed to the spectacular view from above, our expert backcountry pilot, a terrifyingly nonchalant fellow, suddenly dropped the plane down into the river canyon itself, leaving out hearts at a higher altitude.

Swooping and banking like a cliff swallow, we followed the winding contours of Desolation Canyon—the sensation that of riding a sideways roller coaster. Suddenly there was a tiny clearing ahead, not even a real landing strip, just a meadow along the edge of the river where Rock Creek enters the Green, and there we landed, white-knuckled and grateful, with the same sense of giddy relief one feels at the amusement park when the roller coaster finally comes home to dock.

"I don't know why I didn't shoot some film of that," Collector said as we deplaned.

"Because you were paralyzed with terror?" I suggested.

We unloaded the plane and watched a bit wistfully as our pilot took off again. We sure hoped that our outfitters were going to make the rendezvous. We were a long way from nowhere—and they had all the food.

While we waited, we explored Rock Creek. It was a beautiful, idyllic, clear-watered little stream that spilled into the muddy Green River. Len Chmiel broke out a fly rod so that Steve could take some fishing photographs for the magazine. Rock Creek was reported to have some trout in it, but it was so tiny this time of year, barely a trickle, that the fishing seemed problematic, at best. Still, Steve got some good photographs of Len, who was kind of half–real fishing/half–pretend fishing—but looking pretty good while he did so . . . except for this stupid hat that he had insisted upon wearing. The hat was a kind of a narrow-brimmed affair, not exactly a porkpie, but close enough . . . a kind of Art Carney in *The Honeymooners* sort of hat. Steve tried to get Len to take it off for the photo session, but Len refused.

"Are you going to wear that hat for the entire trip?" Steve asked him.

"Why, yes, as a matter of fact I am," said Len. "I like my hat. I just got it."

Unlike the photographer and writer, Len was paying his own way on the trip, and he had clearly not come along to serve as a professional model.

After the fishing shoot, in which Len did not catch any fish, Steve took me aside. "I think we've got a problem," he said.

"What kind of a problem?" I asked.

"A hat problem," he said.

"A hat problem?"

"Yes. If you can't be in any of the pictures," Steve said, "I'm going to have nothing for the magazine beside pictures of Len wearing that stupid hat."

"That's a photographer's problem," I said. "So get him to wear another hat."

"He won't do that," Steve said. "You know Len. What I'm trying to say is that I may have to shoot some photos of you."

"No way. Absolutely not," I insisted. "You'll blow my cover. Remember, the deal is you only shoot me from behind, and sparingly at that."

Even though Collector is an old and dear friend, I didn't altogether trust him on this point. He is, after all, a photographer—an outdoor *paparazzo* of sorts—and I knew that he'd do just about anything to get the shot. It's also quite true that my hat was much better-looking than Len's. I had bought it especially for this trip as part of my disguise—a straw cowboy hat upon which I had done some restyling. It was a hat that I would never wear in my real life—which, of course, made it perfect for an undercover assignment.

Then we spotted our outfitters coming down the river, just as planned. Len's hat was forgotten in the ensuing excitement of introductions, loading of gear and dogs. For dogs we had Len's two perfectly trained (kind of annoyingly so, actually) golden retrievers, Gus and Rusty, Steve's less well trained Brittany, Kate, and, as always, the trusty Sweetz. And we were off.

Via Mastro we had been fortunate to locate a "hunter-friendly" river rafting company in the area. There is, understandably, little crossover between white-water rafting enthusiasts and bird hunters, because so rarely do the twain meet. Indeed, many river runners and outfitters might sneer openly if you told them

that you wished to run the Green not as a white-water experience but in the fall in order to hunt the chukar partridge that inhabit these canyons. Skip Bell, president of Adventure River Expeditions, was the exception. Like all of the other outfitters licensed on the Green, Bell and his staff of experienced boatmen and women ran the river primarily through the highwater spring and summer months. Although not hunters themselves, they couldn't help but notice the chukars down by the river or in the rocks of the canyon walls above, from whence they would hear the distinctive "*chukaring*" sounds issuing. Almost unconsciously they would note the size, number, and location of the various coveys along the river—information of passing interest to river runners but of critical importance to bird hunters.

River rafting business generally drops off as precipitously as water levels by Labor Day, shortly after which chukar season opens. Voilà! The perfect marriage—an opportunity for Bell to both extend his rafting season and share his knowledge of local chukar populations with an appreciative audience. The reason that Skip and his crew had put in two days earlier and floated down to our rendezvous was that the Green River flows through flat farm country in its upper reaches, country of interest neither to chukars nor, consequently, to chukar hunters.

Rounding out Bell's crew were another boatman, named Craig Smith, and a third unexpected staffer by the name of Monte Stadler, who, Bell explained, had been invited along to "guide" us in our chukar-hunting efforts, even though we had not requested a guide. Actually, we learned that Stadler was a big-game outfitter from Alaska and a friend of Bell's and it was clear that he just happened to be visiting at the time of our trip and had been asked along for the ride. Of course we immediately saw through the ruse, because after all, who needs a big-game outfitter from Alaska to guide one on a chukar hunt in Utah? Still we liked Monte right off (his business card read: "*Professional Hunter* Modern Mountain Man**," his telephone number listed as: "*Are you kidding*"?), and we were happy to have him

along; we weren't the kind of demanding clients who might take umbrage at such a tiny liberty as an outfitter inviting a friend on a paid trip. In fact, for the next few days we would even let Monte pretend that he was guiding us—even though we knew just as much, maybe more, about chukar hunting as he did.

But what's more exciting than putting in on the first day of a river trip, with three days of rafting and bird hunting ahead? The country was so wild, so empty, so . . . desolate that as we

pushed off to enter Desolation Canyon itself we couldn't help but feel like explorers ourselves.

Bell had explained to us that the largest chukar concentration were farther yet downriver, in Gray Canyon, and that this first day we would try to make some miles rather than spending a lot of time hunting unproductive country. So we sat back and let the river carry us away.

The Green here has sawed down over the aeons through the high forested Tavaputs Plateau. Above us the Red-striated walls of Desolation Canyon (which, where Rock Creek enters the Green, is deeper than the Grand Canyon) rose hundreds of feet in the air, weathered and sculpted by the river to look like Gothic cathedrals, castles, and turrets; one had an odd sense that this was a place to either worship or pay fealty to, a place for contemplative silence. Where the canyon narrowed the river had carved huge amphitheaters on its curves, creating its own specific world of light and shadow.

As we came around bends in the river, herons and ducks flushed off the water and flew ahead of us or circled around to land again behind us. Way up atop the canyon wall, bighorn sheep stood watching us like Indian sentinels.

We slid past wide sand beaches and lush bottoms of cotton-woods, willows, and box elders—improbable oases in this arid, rocky country. Deer browsed in the bottoms, alert to our passage. A beaver comically dragged home a freshly gnawed cottonwood tree so large that there was some real question about who was dragging whom. Peregrine and prairie falcons peered down from their nests in the cliffs above. There is a quality unique to river trips—a sense of passage, of being brief witness, part of the element while at the same time being borne away by it, both spectator and spectated, a curious sensation that can never be duplicated by highway travel. The dogs slept, curled in their designated spots atop the gear.

Even this time of year, with water levels low, there were periodic stretches of rapids to negotiate. We would be floating at

a perfect snoozing pace down a long muddy slick when we'd hear the distant deeper sound of faster water ahead. Pretty soon we were inside the sound, the river spilling into holes and boiling up over partially exposed rocks. We would take hold of our dogs to secure them and make sure that our waterproof gunslips were properly tied down and ride whooping through the rapids and into the next calm stretch.

So the miles passed. Farther downstream and later in the day we entered Gray Canyon—an appropriate, if unimaginative, choice of names on the part of Powell and his men. But it is quite true that the color of the rock on the canyon walls changed abruptly from the reddish tones of Desolation Canyon to shades of gray—a color, perhaps not coincidentally, that perfectly matched that of the chukar partridge's plumage. It's possible that they do better here simply because they are better camouflaged from predators.

Although we were trying to make some river miles this first day, we couldn't resist stopping occasionally to make short hunts up the side canyons and draws, a kind of warm-up for the rigors ahead.

There exists no more physically demanding form of bird hunting than the pursuit of chukars. At the same time, the people who hunt the species tend toward a certain body and mind type. It's a poor choice of sports for the seriously overweight, the infirm, and heavy smokers. But no matter how good your conditioning, you'll wish you'd spent the whole summer working out on the StairMaster.

Nor is there anything even remotely gentlemanly about the sport—no tradition of walking up at leisure behind elegant points carrying fine shotguns. Serious chukar hunters carry "beater" shotguns that they don't mind getting dinged, scarred, and dented, because sooner or later while scrambling over the rocks you're going to fall down, and when you do you're going to bang the hell out of your shotgun. It's a simple rule of chukar hunting. Here's another: Chukar always run uphill. They

run uphill and fly downhill. And they are built to run in these rocks; with sturdy orange legs and taloned toes they dash up, over, and around the rocks agile as little roadrunners, always seeming to keep a safe distance ahead of the pursuing hunter and his dog, only to finally launch wild off the canyon wall, sailing away to the next canyon over. There's a corny old saying among chukar hunter that you hunt chukars the first time for fun and thereafter for revenge. But personally, I've never held it against the birds.

But this first day we found no chukars, at least not until we had already made camp and Collector and I had quit for the day. Only Len Chmiel, who was the most tireless hunter of our group and who, by rotating his two goldens, effectively doubled his time in the field. Only Len stayed out until nearly dusk, by which time Steve and I were comfortably ensconced in camp chairs having cocktails by the fire, Kate and Sweetz snoozing at our feet. From the plateau above our camp we heard, finally, two quick shots.

Collector laughed and shook his head. "Len's a lunatic," he said. "I knew he'd stay out until he found birds."

Shortly thereafter, Len made his way back to camp. In our camp chairs, cocktails in hand, Collector and I felt a bit like slackers as he approached the fire out of the gathering dark.

"I'll bet you're really curious," Len said, and from his tone we already knew that he had birds in his game bag, that on this, his first chukar hunt, and the first covey of the trip, he had shot a double with his beautiful Purdey twelve gauge. Yes, you heard me correctly—Len is surely the only man in America who has ever hunted wild chukars with a London Best shotgun. I didn't know Len very well at the time, but I know him now, and Steve was right; he is a lunatic. "I'll bet you're *really, really* curious," he said.

"You got into a covey just at dusk and you shot a double," I answered, stealing Len's thunder.

But Len wasn't about to let us off the hook that easily. First

he was going to show us his birds, which he withdrew slowly and with great care from his game bag so that we would really feel like slackers—and possibly rummies, working as we were on our second cocktail—and then he was going to give us the play-by-play description of his hunt. One must allow the successful hunter his recitation—an ancient tradition. So Len poured himself a glass of wine and sat down by the fire.

The next day started kind of slow. We made several stops along the river at places where Skip had seen chukars during the summer, but by midafternoon and after several strenuous forays up side canyons we had yet to locate birds. There was a hint of mutiny in the air. After all, we were a day and a half into a three-day trip, and so far all we had to show for it were Len's two birds. Skip assured us that the prime chukar country was still ahead, but now we were really getting antsy—a variation on the "ugly American" theme; call it the disgruntled sporting client syndrome.

But Captain Bell maintained his equanimity. It takes a specific temperament to be a good outfitter, and Bell had it in spades; he was the picture of serenity and confidence. "Don't worry," he said in response to our whining. "We'll be into the birds soon. Trust me. You'll see plenty of birds before we're finished."

And as if on cue, while we floated serenely through a long, slow slick, someone of the group picked up the faint but distinctive sound of chukars calling from the rocks above the river—*chukar-chukar-chukar*—pretty soon everyone heard it, a growing chorus rising from the canyon. Now the adrenaline began to flow. The boatmen found a spot to beach the boats, and everyone piled out—a melee of hunters and dogs, assembling guns and gear. Right off, the dogs had scent, which only served to increase the general excitement.

We were hardly away from the boats when chukars started

rocketing off the rocks above us, busted by one or another of our dogs. Sweetz was an old hand at chukar hunting and loved nothing more than running them down in the rocks and pushing them up into the air. Due to the birds' propensity to run, rather than hold for a point, flushing dogs are often more effective than pointers on chukars.

Now birds spilled off the rocks above us, at odd tangents and angles. There is nothing quite like chukar hunting for presenting a variety of peculiar shots. Collector was standing behind me, and he started hollering and pointing at birds for me to shoot. I turned and swung on a bird that flew high over my head and headed out over the river. It was like a pass shot on high ducks. "Shoot it!" Steve hollered.

Steve and I have known each other for years, have been on numerous magazine assignments together, and are the best of friends, but sometimes we get on each other's nerves. For Steve's part, as an avid hunter and fisherman himself, it is often a source of great frustration to be always carrying his camera rather than a fly rod or shotgun. For my part, it is sometimes a source of irritation to have him skulking around behind me all the time, offering lots of unsolicited advice while pointing his camera in my face. I have difficulty enough with my shooting and casting.

But I killed the bird as it flew out over the river, and it dropped into the water and began to float away in the current. Sweetz had seen the chukar fall, and she scrambled down off the rocky slope to the river's edge, where she leaped off a rock into the water. Her water entry was as perfectly executed as a dog food commercial, and now she swam intently, one thing in her little Lab mind—to gather that bird in her mouth. Cleverly Sweetz angled with the current to intercept the drifting chukar, snatched it up, and swam back to shore. I was mightily proud of her.

I turned to Collector. "Did you get some great shots of that?" I asked.

And Steve looked suddenly crestfallen and a bit befuddled. He looked down at his empty hands. "I don't have my camera," he said, as if he had just noticed this fact.

"You don't have your camera?" I asked incredulously. "My dog just made one of the great retrieves of her life and you don't have your camera?"

"I got so caught up in the action," he said, "that I forgot to pick it up."

"Maybe if you spent less time instructing me on my shooting," I said crankily, "you'd have more time to concentrate on doing your job."

"I thought I wasn't supposed to be shooting you anyway," Collector pointed out. "Remember? You and Sweetz are under-cover."

Steve and I sometimes remind me of a couple of old spinster sisters. But I had to admit he had a point, and in any case, now that we had located birds our minor tiff was quickly forgotten. Steve grabbed his camera, and we hunters headed off to work our way up the various side canyons that ran like knurled arthritic fingers to the river. There seemed to be birds everywhere; we could hear their calls echoing off the canyon walls as if in an amphitheater, so that the sound was hard to pinpoint, birds everywhere, the canyon full of chukars, and we chased them up, up, up. Sometimes we could see them squirting through the rocks ahead of us, and then just as suddenly they would seem to vanish, to disappear as if they had become rocks themselves. And sometimes Sweetz would put up a bunch and I'd have wonderful shooting—strange shooting, sometimes downhill toward the river, sometimes cross-canyon, always off-balance . . . coveys of chukars coming off the rock faces of the canyon walls like dynamite explosions . . . birds coming out of the shadows of the canyon and flying through the sunlight and back into the shadows on the other side . . . a world of light and shadow, gray birds against gray rock, flashes of black-barred breasts, pinpoints of orange beak and orange legs. There is simply no stranger or more

wonderful form of bird shooting, in stranger or more wonderful country, than chukar hunting.

And from the other canyon fingers came the muffled sounds of gunfire from my confederates, so I knew that they, too, were into birds. And we climbed and climbed and climbed, and sometimes we would catch sight of one another on a distant ledge. No matter how hard I climbed, I always noticed that Monte, who had a mountain goat–like build with a low center of gravity and legs like pistons, was one ridge higher.

Only Capt. Skip Bell stayed back with the boats, relaxing and enjoying the often-amusing spectacle of birds bailing off the cliffs as off-kilter gunners peppered the rocks or laced the skies with birdshot. Often we couldn't even see the birds, and Skip, with the best seat in the house, would chuckle to himself as he watched them run out ahead of us, to crest a ridge and then sail off unmolested to the next ridge over.

The weather was unseasonably hot, and I was hunting in shorts, which was a decided trade-off when wading through the thorny brush along the river's edge or when I slipped in the rocks. By the end of the trip my legs would look like they had been lashed by bamboo switches. Sweetz is a better athlete by far, with better balance and, of course, four feet, and while she didn't fall down, the rocks were hard on her paws. Stupidly I had neglected to boot her, and by the end of the trip her pads would be so raw and tender that it would be painful for her to walk for several days. I had never booted her before and was unaware of the fact that a dog's pads are a lot like four-by-four truck tires. They do not get callused and tougher with time but thinner with age. Sweetz's had a lot of hard miles on them, and the tread was simply wearing down, and I realize that I should have started booting her earlier in her career, for which oversight I still lose sleep at night.

By midday the canyons were like convection ovens, and one thing I wasn't going to do was kill my dog with heat prostration—to which Labs are more prone than any other sporting

breed. I carried two plastic water bottles in my game belt, but after the strenuous climb and with a few birds in the bag we made our way back down to the river, where I found a cool back-eddy for Sweetz to paddle around in.

After all the hunters had regrouped at the boats and re-counted their respective adventures, compared and admired one another's birds, we loaded back up and went around the corner, just downriver, to that night's campsite in a spot called Rattle-snake Canyon. It was here in the winter of 1899–1900 that the Wild Bunch outlaw Flat Nose George Curry (so named after having been kicked flush in the face by a horse) had lived in a cave while building a raft to make good his escape down the Green River. But before Curry could finish his raft he was cor-nered by two posses here in Rattlesnake Canyon and shot to death in a hail of gunfire.

We took a brief rest before making a final late-afternoon hunt. This time, Collector couldn't resist swapping his camera for a shotgun. I headed down the river bottom while Steve climbed the canyon. Some time later I looked up to see him and Kate on top of the plateau hundreds of feet above the river. It gave me vertigo just to look at them up there, and then I heard Collector give a kind of wild man call, part Tyrolean yodel, part Tarzan, part primal scream, pure joy.

Later everyone would reconnoiter back at the night's camp—which, conveniently, our outfitters had set up while we were hunting. They had a good fire burning, dinner was being prepped, and all the fixings for cocktails had been set out on the folding kitchen table. The hunters made themselves drinks, and everyone sat down in camp chairs to rest their weary bones while exhausted dogs flopped like corpses in the sand at our feet.

Postscript

E-mail message from editor at *Outdoor Life:* "Jim. Just out of curiosity was that you and Sweetzer plastered all over the cover of this month's *Sports Afield?*"

7

OF FLUSHING MULES
AND PRAIRIE TUNA

Pinnated Grouse
Latin name: Tympanuchus cupido (Linnaeus) 1758
Other vernacular names: Prairie chicken, prairie cock, prairie
grouse, prairie hen; cupidon des prairies, poule des prairies
(French); Eigentliche Prariehuhn (German)
          —Paul A. Johnsgard, *The Grouse of the World*

        —aka prairie tuna
        Fergus/Valdene/Stanton (1996)

"The only thing you want to watch out for with Badger," says mule skinner Bob Mark, who in his free time is a school shop teacher and part-time contractor from North Platte, Nebraska, "is that if he gets to galloping, sometimes he doesn't respond very well to the 'whoa' command.

"You have to grab the reins and kind of pump like this," he adds, demonstrating a series of quick, serious jerks.

"Who said anything about galloping?" I answer. If I were interested in speed, I'd be riding an ATV rather than a donkey-horse hybrid, and under the circumstances I'm very happy to be plodding across the Nebraska prairie at a brisk walk atop my trusty roan jack (a male mule) Badger, whose big ears flop pleasantly in tune with his gait.

Although I have ridden horses on and off all my life and have even owned a few over the years, I've always had a somewhat uneasy relationship with the beasts. What I know about them is that they are big and strong and dumb and capable of wreaking an enormous amount of havoc, not to mention physical injury, upon the relatively puny human being. In fact, it's taken me better than forty years to finally realize that I just don't much care for horses.

But these mules are something else altogether, and right from the start I find myself bonding with old Badger. He has already sized me up as a dude, but he doesn't hold that against me the way that a horse will, nor does he try to take advantage of the fact. And he steps out right smartly with a smooth, easy gait, which, because mules are narrower in the withers than horses, doesn't leave the rider feeling at the end of the day like he's been working out for eight consecutive hours with Suzanne Somers's Thigh-master. (Look; there's a reason that cowboys walk that way.)

"Mules have gotten a bum rap over the years," explains Mark, a large, substantial man with red hair and beard, a wry sense of humor, and arms stout as corner posts. "People have this idea that they're mean and stubborn, prone to kick and bite, but in many ways they're a lot smarter and more gentle than horses, and if they're trained right you can do things with them that just you can't do on a horse."

"Like shoot off them?" one of our group asks.

"Oh, sure," Bob answers, deadpan. "You can do that . . . at least once."

Actually, the plan is not to shoot off the backs of the mules but simply use them as transportation to locate birds. This is

real big country that can make a hunter on foot feel mighty small and helpless, and these mules can eat up the ground for you.

Joining me and photographer Steve Collector on this expedition in the prairie sandhills outside the tiny, hospitable hamlet of Wallace, Nebraska, are our painter friend Len Chmiel (surely the only man in America who has hunted chukars in Utah canyon country *and* prairie chickens on mules with an English Purdy twelve-gauge double shotgun) and advertising art director Michael Hall from Denver, who shoots a twelve-gauge Beretta auto-loader. Both have good dogs—Chmiel now with a trio of impeccably trained golden retrievers (Gus, Rusty, and Diva) and Hall a fine young Brittany, named Belle—and both are excellent shots. Collector also has his Brittany, Kate, along. And, naturally, I have Sweetz.

One of the most valuable things that donkey blood adds to the horse gene pool, we soon discover, is the ability to jump barbwire fences from a standstill. We dismount, and Mark wraps a piece of cloth around the top two strands and issues the command, *"Heap, heap."* (Bob doesn't know where this time-honored mule-skinner command originated, but possibly it is simply a melding of the words *hop* and *leap*.) And over they go—jumping jacks and jennies (a jenny, of course, being a female mule).

So now we are strung out across the prairie, a long line of mules and riders, six of us all together, shotguns in scabbards at our side, sundry dogs working the hills for birds or trotting along at heel. It's the first time Sweetz, or any of the other dogs for that matter, has ever heeled beside or hunted in front of a mule, and the fact that their respective hunting partners are way up higher than usual is cause for a certain canine disorientation. Until they gradually become accustomed to our new position the dogs spend a lot of time running comically from mule to mule looking at the wrong eye-level for their masters. "Yo,

Sweetz," I have to keep reminding her with a wave. "I'm up here."

For some reason the dogs are surprisingly unintimidated by the mules and run right through their legs or, during our frequent rest stops, flop at their feet trying to score some shade— a rare commodity on the prairie. For their part, the mules, who have logged hundreds of hours in the company of Bob's and his partner Leon's coon hounds, seem pretty much oblivious to our dogs—but actually go out of their way not to step on them.

Only one . . . well, two canine/equine mishaps will mar the trip, and that is when the newest mule in Mark's string, a chestnut jenny named, perhaps inappropriately, Easy, sucker-punches Mike Hall's Brittany, Belle, twice—once on two successive days. Both times the dog makes the same mistake of putting her nose up against Easy's rear hock as if trying to sniff out her master on top. And both times the kick, which is the lightning-fast mule equivalent of the young Ali's jab, catches Belle in the exact same spot square on the snout—makes a sickening hollow cracking sound. The dog squeals bloody murder and runs around in a circle, weaving like a punch-drunk fighter before finally going down for the count. Fortunately, no lasting harm is done and an hour later Belle, with a small lump on her nose, is hunting again as if nothing at all has happened.

It is a bizarre leap of taxonomic classification, I know. But maybe it was the illusion of being on a ship at sea, a common-enough hallucination among pioneers on the Great Plains (who went so far as to refer to their wagons as "prairie schooners"), that first put me in mind of tuna—the swells of prairie running off to the skyline, the gentle bobbing of the mules not unlike the feeling of being jostled on a choppy ocean. In fact, a certain region of the Nebraska sandhills is referred to as the "sand choppies" and resembles nothing so much as a rough sea on the

horizon—even seems to move like waves in a shimmering heat-induced optical illusion.

And the birds themselves kicked up ahead of our noble mounts, set their short curved grouse wings like small lateral fins, and sailed away like schools of plump fish. . . . But mostly, it was the deep pink shade of the prairie chicken's breast meat, which bears a far greater resemblance to the raw red tuna favored in sushi bars than it does to the anemically pale domestic chicken meat (and, unless properly aged and prepared, can taste a bit like tuna, too, I'm afraid).

The prairie chicken (of which there are three subspecies still extant in North America—greater, lesser, and Attwater—and a fourth extinct since 1932: the eastern heath hen) was once, arguably, the most prolific game bird on earth; its range stretched north to south from Canada to Texas and east to west from Ohio to eastern Colorado and New Mexico. Accounts by early settlers describe huge flocks of thousands, collectively millions of birds. In A Sand County Almanac, Aldo Leopold tells of the year 1873, when the Chicago markets purchased 600,000 prairie chickens from market gunners.

Today there aren't that many prairie chickens left on the entire continent—not even close. As grouse expert Paul A. Johnsgard points out, the pinnated grouse is "the species that has been most affected by human activities in North America." Although market hunting took an obvious toll on bird populations, the primary cause for the precipitous decline of the prairie chicken was the plowing of the virgin prairies and the subsequent conversion of grasslands to cultivated croplands. Thus by the early part of the twentieth century the pinnated grouse had already been extirpated from much of its historical range and greatly reduced in numbers in all of the rest.

The good news is that the prairie chicken has survived in several Great Plains states, and though its populations may never again approach the prolificacy of the past century, some states, including Nebraska, still maintain stable, huntable pop-

ulations of birds. Over the years the species has been adaptable enough to add cultivated grains and grasses—primarily corn, wheat, and alfalfa—to diet, and in the region of the state that we are hunting, the introduction of the center pivot irrigation system over the past two decades may actually have increased prairie chicken numbers. But more is clearly not better; research indicates that regardless of the availability of food, the bird can not survive if more than 60 percent of its native grassland prairie is destroyed.

"You want to watch out for orange flags in the corners of the pivot fields," explains Leon Fanning, our other professional mule man, Bob Mark's friend and coon-hunting partner (for which pursuit they also ride mules, sometimes all night and well into the wee hours of the morning). "They put them up after they spray the corn. The flags have forty-eight-or seventy-two-hour expiration dates on the back. That's when they say it's safe for human beings to enter the area without the protection of full-body suits." Leon, a lean, competent, soft-spoken fellow, whose slight accent betrays his Missouri roots, shakes his head at the insanity of this situation. As a utilities company lineman, fore-man of the local Rural Electric Association, Fanning is some-times called upon to enter these "hot" zones. And as the father of four young children he, like many of his rural neighbors, is understandably concerned about the future of chemically sup-ported agriculture. So polluted from agricultural run-off are some wells and aquifers in Nebraska that there are entire towns where children under a certain age, elderly people, and those with health problems are warned against drinking the water. So much for the national fantasy of living the healthful life on the family farm.

Which is not to say that we as hunters—opportunists—do not hunt the grassy, weedy corners of the pivot fields where birds seek cover, though after Leon's warning we keep an eye out for orange flags. At the same time, this is a bit too much like pheas-ant hunting for my tastes, and the sandburrs—the first insidious

invaders when the prairie sod is turned over by the plow—are particularly fierce this year and make for difficult hunting conditions for the dogs, even though we have them booted (a virtual necessity, by the way, in this country).

No, what I like best is being at large in the shortgrass prairie itself, riding the hills and draws on old Badger, seeing land that is very little changed from what it must have looked like a couple of hundred years ago.

"The ranchers often don't get enough credit for restoring the native grasslands," explains Bob Mark as we ride out across this rolling prairie. "They've really done an excellent job of it. They could easily graze this land into oblivion. But they're very careful about rotating their cattle, and they've put in stock wells so that they can rotate more frequently. The prairie is healthier now than it's ever been."

We are hunting on land that belongs to a man named Lynn Frederick, a friendly, generous, inquisitive third-generation rancher, who comes out to visit with us each morning in the ranch yard as Bob and Leon saddle the mules and again in the evening after the hunt, when our seemingly tireless hosts unsaddle and curry our mounts while we sports flop around in the shade with our exhausted dogs. (We do what we can to help, but the mule skinners have long since figured out that their own routine is more efficient without a bunch of dudes mucking up the procedure.) We munch apples picked from the overgrown orchard of an old abandoned homestead we came upon in the prairie, drink soda pop, and relive the day's adventures. Lynn usually has his towheaded two-year-old son, Landon, with him and tells us tales of his father and grandfather, thus connecting the generations, and peripherally us, to this fine country of prairie and sky.

Frederick is proud of his stewardship of the land, as well he should be. The past summer had been unusually wet in Nebraska, and the early-fall weather mild, so that the mixed prairie grasses are still astonishingly green, peppered with bunches of

red-tinted bluestem and wispy silvery prairie sage. The ranch offers spectacular bird habitat, with plenty of food and cover, and we are not disappointed in our quest.

Sometimes we ride right up on the birds before they flush, and sometimes they get up wild in large coveys a couple of hundred yards away. In either case, these prairie tuna are built to fly, and we watch them sail away in the vast sea of sky until they are mere specks on the horizon, cresting the distant hills and setting their wings, to come down, we hope, on the other side, the coveys split up now and spread out across the prairie hillsides.

Thus scattered, the birds tend to hold better for the dogs, and we ride over to the general vicinity in which we saw them down and slip off our faithful mounts. We slide guns from scabbards and either hand our lead ropes to Bob or Leon or else hook them to our belt loops (not, we are strongly advised, to the belts themselves in case something should cause our mules to blow up, in which event we will definitely prefer the quick-release option of a torn belt loop to being more permanently tethered to 800-plus pounds of exploding muleflesh).

Now the hunters spread out on foot, working the hills and the "blowouts." These latter are areas in which the fragile grass covering has been disturbed, usually by either fire or cattle or truck tires, and from which the sand has then been scoured by the wind, forming a small craterlike depression in the earth. Either naturally or by the restorative efforts of conscientious ranchers like Lynn Frederick, many of these blowouts are eventually reseeded, and prairie chickens like them for the good cover and shelter from the wind that they provide.

As we walk the hills, guns in the ready position, meadowlarks sing and flush out around us and crickets hum in a rising tuning fork–like crescendo that seems to foreshadow some drama to come.

The dogs work out ahead as our mules follow placidly behind;

we disappear into the troughs of swells, to reappear for a moment on the crest before dropping into the next. Now the prairie tuna are vaulting up out of the grass in singles, pairs, and small coveys. And the shooting begins. Maybe the wind is blowing—it usually is on the prairie—and sometimes the shots of our companions, though close by, are snatched away so that they seem no louder than cap guns. Here and there we see a small burst of feathers, birds tumbling from the sky, dogs running for retrieves, our gentle mules taking all the natural tumult of the prairie in perfect stride.

8

YAAK MAGIC

I love the symphony and magic of the deep woods best. . . . It is
dark here and rains a lot and the trees are big and there are
mysterious assemblages of animals, groupings and relationships
found nowhere else in the world. It is my home.
—Rick Bass, *The Book of Yaak*

My friend Guy de la Valdène and I had been hunting chukars
on the breaks of the Grande Ronde River in eastern Washington
State late one September. It was country of enormous grandeur,
of vast benches above winding canyons, shadowed hills rising to
mountains, deep canyons falling away forever to the river below.
Where we hunted up high, it was the sort of big, open country
that gave you a kind of pit-in-the-stomach thrill, nearly a quea-
siness.

We each had our own vehicle and had driven in tandem
straight from Washington, where it was hot, dry, and bright, to
Montana's Yaak valley, which has the feel of a Pacific Northwest
rain forest and where a cold front with rain and fog and low

dark clouds had settled in over the lush, dark-timbered woods. We had come to visit and bird-hunt with the writer Rick Bass.

Sometimes going too quickly from one country to another can be unsettling, as if the afterimage of the country you have just left behind is still burned upon your mind's eye and the new country seems somehow alien and inhospitable or, worse, malevolent. At the same time, for those of us sensitive to country (and most hunters are), certain topographies and climates can serve as triggers to the imagination and memory. In this manner a deep sense of dread had fallen upon Guy as pervasively as the black storm clouds that hung over the woods of the Yaak. "I don't think I can stay here long," he said to me shortly after we arrived. "I don't like this country; it makes me uneasy." The mountains hereabouts did seem a bit close, tightly set and heavily forested (that is, where they had not been scalped on top in vast bleak tracks of clear-cuts). In fact, it was hard to see why they even called this a valley, and I, too, found it a bit claustrophobic at first, especially with the low sky closing in from above.

"Well, it is a little gloomy," I admitted. "But you can't leave yet. We have a date to hunt with Bass tomorrow."

"I'll see how I feel in the morning," Guy said. "But I may have to get out of these woods."

"Maybe it'll clear up tomorrow," I suggested. "A little sun could make all the difference in the world."

But it didn't clear up, and the next morning's late dawn was even gloomier—colder and darker and still drizzling steadily. Guy was staying in a bed and breakfast on the edge of the tiny town of Yaak, which was little more than a crossroads, with a couple of bars on either side of the street and a mercantile, and I was camped out back in the Airstream. First thing that morning he knocked on my door. "I'm leaving," he announced. "Are you coming?"

"Gee," I said, indecisively, "I don't know; I came all the way

up here to hunt with Bass. I made a date with him. I just don't feel that I should leave."

"That's all right," Guy said, "but I really do have to go."

It is said that the Yaak is a place of magic, and where there is magic must also lurk its evil twin, black magic, and perhaps this is what had so affected de la Valdène, for I had never seen him spooked like that, almost frightened, and he is one of the bravest men I know.

"I hate for us to split up now," I said. "It's only for one day. We can both leave tomorrow."

"No, I have to leave right now," Guy insisted. "This country reminds me too much of Switzerland." He hesitated and added almost apologetically, "It looks just like the place in Switzerland where my father died."

I understood; certain country holds our ghosts, and sometimes you just have to get in the car and drive a couple of hundred miles to escape them. So Guy and I said our good-byes; I was sorry to see him go. Right after he left, as the dark clouds descended even farther upon the forest and the rain ticked steadily against the aluminum shell of the Airstream, I wished that I had gone with him. I envied him the big open plains of eastern Montana toward which he was headed. I turned the furnace up higher, poured another cup of coffee, and went to scribbling in my notebook.

The rain had abated to a misting drizzle by the time Rick Bass met me at the Airstream for our hunt. The Yaak is Bass's home country, and anyone familiar with his work will know how much he loves it. Just as this country filled Guy with apprehension, so it fills Bass with wonder, reverence, and joy. The same sense of mystery and import that seems palpable in the damp, dark woods and mountains of the Yaak inhabits Bass's fiction, where magical occurrences become almost commonplace and where characters,

both human and animal, are frequently capable of feats of strength and endurance possible only in a magical land.

Bass is a quiet, shy, watchful, intensely polite man with large, expressive, almost alarmingly bright blue eyes, eyes that own an innate, animal-like alertness. He had his German shorthair, Colter, with him, and we all loaded up in my Suburban and headed for the first covert of the day.

There was still plenty of green in the woods, but the aspens and cottonwoods were beginning to turn various shades of yellow, orange, and red. The snowberries were white upon the bush, and the berries on the kinnikinnick a deep red. There were larch trees and alder, fir, and spruce, a diversity and lushness to which I was unaccustomed. And there was a strange stillness about the forest, the earth lying somber under its shroud of clouds.

I liked hunting with Bass right off. He's a walker—a careful, attentive hunter, who seems to absorb the land as he moves through it. And he knows his country. Sweetz and Colter worked well together, too, Colter ranging a good deal farther out, Sweetz working close. "Do you ever get lost in the woods around here?" I asked Rick, because it struck me immediately that this was the kind of country in which I'd have been instantly and hopelessly lost if hunting alone. To be honest, I'm a little afraid of the deep woods.

"Oh, sure," he said. He paused and seemed to consider the question. "Sometimes I get so lost," he added, "that I don't know where I am." It was a classic Rick Bass remark, slightly off-center but right on the money, and though I had to think about it for a moment, I knew just what he meant: there's lost, and then there's *lost*.

Just then Sweetz got birdy—nose to the ground, snuffling, tail wagging stiffly—and suddenly she put up a ruffed grouse. I mounted my gun and fired. The grouse vanished in the woods. "I sure shot hell out of that tree," I said of the tree that stood

between me and the unscathed bird. I rarely hit anything when hunting in the forest, either.

We hunted on. Every now and then I would look over at Bass as we walked through a covert. He was always smiling to himself, as if in pure conscious joy at being alive at this moment, being right here in the country that he loved so, doing what we were doing, a smile of pleasure and gratitude that couldn't help but make the visitor feel good about things.

Those who know Rick Bass's work will also be familiar with his legendary efforts to preserve the wildness of the Yaak Valley. A one-man crusader and activist, he has taken on the logging companies, lobbied state and federal politicians, and written hundreds of impassioned letters, editorials, and magazine pieces and a book (*The Book of the Yaak*) to rally support for the Yaak. He brings to his preservation efforts a conviction that is nearly religious, evangelical, a quality that one finds in his use of language and in his voice as well. Indeed, I know of no other writer whose spoken voice is so similar to, and inseparable from, his written voice. "Look at that aspen tree," he will say of a particularly vibrantly colored tree, as if he's never seen one before. "It's almost nourishing, like a meal."

We hunted on, working out each of Bass's coverts and then going back to the vehicle to drive through the woods to another. Sweetz and Colter were hunting well and put up several birds for us. At one point, Sweetz flushed a spruce grouse, but it only fluttered up to the nearest tree branch, allowing me to walk over and look it right in its red eye. Spruce grouse was one of the handful of American upland game bird species that Sweetz had not retrieved in her career, but of course we don't shoot birds out of trees. We hunted on.

The drizzling rain continued. "Look at that," Bass said of a bank of thick clouds drifting over the mountainside. "It's so beautiful." It was as if he were seeing the country for the first time, seeing it through the eyes of his visitor. Bass told me a

story about a mountain lion chasing his dog and of his own sense of fear, anger, and exhilaration in witnessing the scene. He told me bear stories and wolf stories. This is clearly a man who spends a great deal of his time in the woods and pays attention.

It's an odd thing, but I remember nearly all the details of that day. I remember very clearly the grouse Sweetz and Colter pointed or flushed, as the case might be, and even how each bird flew through the woods. I remember the country and the weather and sitting in the steamy Suburban in between coverts as the rain fell outside and filling our coffee cups from a thermos. "Doesn't that smell great?" Bass said. I remember that my other dog, a part dachsund/part terrier mix named Betty, who is Sweetz's and my frequent traveling companion and who does not get much ink in these pages because she isn't a bird dog, struck up a little innocent flirtation with Colter in the back of the Suburban. All this I remember, but I can't remember if we killed any birds. I don't think we did, but I just don't remember exactly. I do remember that we had one of those rare perfect days, when the dogs were brilliant and the country revealed just enough of itself to keep things interesting.

And I remember this: We were driving out on the highway after hunting our final covert of the day, headed for the tavern in town (both taverns, actually, as Bass can hardly patronize one without also crossing the street to have a beer in the other). We were driving through the forest, and I turned to say something to Rick, and in that split second before I turned my eyes back to the road a deer materialized directly in front of the vehicle. There she stood, a doe, ears pricked forward, staring at us in frozen silhouette as we bore down upon her. I slammed on the brakes and the Suburban came to an immediate halt. I don't mean that it screeched to a stop; I mean it just *stopped*, right there, dead in its tracks. The doe bounded across the road and disappeared into the forest.

"I was certain that you were going to hit that deer," Bass said. "I've never seen a truck come to a stop like that."

"Yeah, well, I just had the brake pads replaced," I answered lamely.

But we both knew that new brake pads had nothing to do with it. It was a simple case of Yaak magic.

9

WAY NORTH

The fine sand of the Nebraska sandhills blew like a vapor across the highway, a narrow road that rose and fell on the swells of land. A blond cowgirl in an old flesh-colored Plymouth sedan sped past me, then a black man with a six-point deer strapped to the roof rack of his sport utility vehicle. It was the day of the Million Man March in Washington, D.C., and I thought it was a fine thing that this fellow was taking a deer home to his family.

The old highway ran alongside the new—whole sections of it having been sloughed off into great craters by the shifting sands, testament to the impermanence of man's place in this country.

A gusting headwind caught the rig at the top of the hills and threatened to push us backward. Even with the accelerator held to the floor, I couldn't get the speedometer over fifty mph; traveling with the Airstream in tow, I've learned that it's best to plan on arriving whenever you arrive. We were headed to North Dakota for a goose hunt, but what was the big rush?

The night before, I had camped in the city park of tiny Stapleton, Nebraska. It was a nice, clean, quiet park, and I had it to myself. That morning over breakfast at the Shady Lady Cafe, festively decorated for Halloween, I overheard concerned townsfolk discussing a recent robbery. It seems that a young man from North Platte drove up here, broke in the garage across the street, and stole five tires. Then he broke into the VFW Club and stole all their Budweiser. Much speculation was made over this last fact: the discriminating thief left behind all the Miller products and only stole those of Anheuser-Busch. Clearly he considered himself to be strictly a Bud man. And the fact that he stole a specific number of tires—five—suggests that he was taking them for his own vehicle and wanted a matching spare. Only a few years ago robberies were unheard of in Stapleton, and the young man from the "city" probably thought he could get away with a middle-of-the-night heist in the hinterlands, but they caught him the very next day.

Across the Loup River, the South Loup, the North Loup, bucking the headwind all day long, so that we only made it as far as Herreid, South Dakota (pop. 488), by nightfall and again camped in the park there. Many of the rural towns around which I bird-hunt in the fall are so small that they have don't have motels or even RV parks. But nearly all of them, no matter how tiny, take pride in having clean, well-maintained town parks where overnight camping is generally allowed, and often there's no charge for the privilege. Many of the parks have electric and water hook-up available, or at least a water spigot to fill your tank. By way of paying back, in some small measure, the hospitality of these fine little communities, I try to leave a few dollars behind—by buying a tank of gas at the local station or some groceries at the market or having breakfast in the café or a beer in the tavern. If possible, I make a small contribution to the town's "park fund."

Leaving Herreid in the morning, black storm clouds massing

to the north, the wind steady at 30–40 mph, gusting as high as 55, I computed that were it not for the headwind holding me back, I would be doing 105 mph easy.

The commodity prices played on the radio station—November wheat, December soybeans, January hogs, February pork bellies. *"In a moment we'll visit Crofton, Nebraska, and talk about feeder pigs,"* said the local radio announcer. Over the border and through the tiny farm town of Strasburg, North Dakota, a sign proudly proclaiming it to be the birthplace of Lawrence Welk, with an arrow pointing toward the Lawrence Welk farmhouse. Tempting, to be sure, but on I drove. Maybe next time.

I knew I was getting way north when I picked up a radio station in Saskatchewan, today's show devoted to Gamblers Anonymous confessionals: among them a heartbreaking story from a wheat farmer's wife who, unknown to her husband, had mortgaged the farm to support her habit and, of course, lost everything. I changed the station again and this time found and listened to a full half-hour interview with a chiropractor on the proper posture and technique for raking leaves and shoveling snow. Only in the north country.

I finally reached Kramer, North Dakota, my destination, at dusk of a cold, wet, windy evening. If you're a bird hunter you've probably been in, or at least through, dozens of such hamlets in the Great Plains. They look like partial ghost towns, most of the storefronts on Main Street boarded up. Those that aren't have broken windows and dust swirled on the floor and maybe a few unwanted items left behind by the former tenants. On the edge of town are the railroad tracks and the agricultural co-op with the grain storage bins towering like cathedrals—which in a sense they are—sad reminders of an ancient dead religion. For in many cases modern agricultural has betrayed the faith of the local populace, whose smaller places have been absorbed by the larger—by the inexorable forces of global markets and agribusiness.

In this particular town even the local elementary school had

gone out of business, as declining rural populations have similarly forced many small schools in the Great Plains to consolidate or be absorbed by larger towns. Usually there just aren't enough kids left in town to attend them. It says something, certainly, about the sociology and demographics of a region when the last two going concerns in the village are the local saloon and the senior citizen center.

In this case, the former elementary school had been recycled by a duck-and-goose-hunting outfitter into a kind of barebones hunting camp. The outfitter bought the place cheap because there's not much of a market for defunct school buildings. These days hunting often offers one of the last economic lights in these otherwise-dimming towns.

I had no trouble at all finding the school; it was right in the middle of town and, to be sure, still looked a lot more like a school than it would ever look like a hunting lodge—it was long and low, with brick facing around the base and large aluminum-framed windows. Inside, the hallways had that same hollow feel when you walked down them and harsh fluorescent lights hummed from the ceiling.

The goose hunters were put up dormitory-style on cots in the classrooms, and blackboards hung on the wall with some forever-unsolved algebra problems that no one ever bothered to erase still chalked upon them. I never did well in math, and I still didn't know the answers to these equations.

I was grateful, as always, to be staying in the Airstream, which was parked out back in the schoolyard. I hadn't much liked school the first time around, and the atmosphere here only increased my feeling of autumnal melancholy.

The stage in the auditorium/gymnasium served as the lodge dining room, as if the diners were actors in a crummy school production. That first night, and the previous one, too, by all accounts, the *spécialité de maison* was another old school standby—mystery meat with a brown sauce cooked for countless hours in a Crock-Pot. "Brown food," my friend Oliver Moore

called it. Like the unanswered algebra questions, I had a hunch that this dish might also have been left over from days gone by. I put the top back on the Crock-Pot and peered into the next. Same stuff—more brown food—not a vegetable in sight, just some institutional rolls, a dish of butter pads, and a tray of half-pint cartons of whole milk. . . . In the refrigerator of the Airstream I had a full head of romaine lettuce, which suddenly seemed as precious as gold bullion. I'll bet I could sell it to this group for ten bucks. Some of the goose hunters had been here for a week and, to my mind, were already displaying signs of scurvy.

I was sitting at a folding dining table with Moore and my Englishman friend Douglas Tate. Furtively I launched a pad of butter from the end of my spoon toward the ceiling. Clearly the school atmosphere was having a strange effect on me; I had the insane desire to start a food fight, in which case I'd only get myself sent to the principal's office.

After dinner, Doug, Oliver, and I drove section roads, perfectly straight, to the nearby town of Newburg. It has always seemed to me that when they were laying this Great Plains farm country out they should have put some more curves in the road just for the sake of variety. The monotony of straight roads numbs the human imagination.

Newburg looked remarkably like Kramer. Had the same ubiquitous grain elevators by the railroad track and was also mostly abandoned and boarded up, except for the village bar, which tonight was offering special entertainment for the visiting army of goose hunters that had occupied the region. But it was early yet and there were mainly ranch vehicles parked in front, and when we entered the establishment we found that we were the only goose hunters in attendance. Rather, a number of local men sat drinking beer at the bar and at the tables as they waited for the evening show to begin; they wore farm implement caps and glanced about furtively, as if they might be worried about being caught here by their wives.

The entertainment tonight was in the form of a couple of "exotic" dancers (God, I love that term) from Minot, North Dakota, the region's hub. At the appointed time a piece of plywood was placed over the pool table and the first dancer, a short, plump blond girl built like a "brick shithouse," as they say in the country, pranced out to the tinny strains of Bonnie Raitt singing on the jukebox. The girl climbed up on the makeshift stage and launched into an energetic, if distinctly unsensuous, dance routine. Perhaps because this was, after all, the heartland there was a certain innocence to the scene that was not at all tawdry, not at all like strip joints in the city. Even the dancers looked innocent—just a couple of farm girls from Minot (itself hardly a Sodom or Gomorrah) trying to make a buck. Who could blame them?

In fact, when you come right down to it there is no blame to be laid anywhere for the death of small towns, the failure of the family farm, the transition of entire regions from this to that, to whatever they happen to become. It's simply the way things are and have always been. Just ask the Indians.

After the chunky blonde had finished her set, she climbed down to work the crowd for tips, replaced on the pool table by her compatriot, a pretty, slender, dark-haired young woman who danced with considerably less enthusiasm, as if she didn't really enjoy her job.

Meanwhile the blonde made her rounds, as inexorable as a bill collector: she grasped the men, one by one, in bear hugs, kissed their faces with pouty lips, whispered in their ears, pressing her ample breasts against their chests. Then she would pull her G-string out just far enough to offer them a tiny peek at her treasures and a natural spot to tuck their dollar bills. When she reached our threesome, Douglas Tate leaped nervously from his stool and scurried around to hide behind the bar.

"I *cannot* do it," Douglas said in his distinctive Geordie (prounounced–"jordy") accent. (For all you Anglophiles, Robert McNeil, in his fascinating book *The Story of English*, called the

Geordie the most popular regional accent in Britain.) "I'm English!"

Being good Americans, both Moore and I meekly submitted to the girl's manhandling and at the proper moment dutifully deposited our bills. "You may as well come out and take your medicine now, Douglas," Oliver said.

Indeed, the little exotic dancer was not to be denied; no patron would be left unassaulted, and when Tate took a tentative step forward she was on him like a pro wrestler making a preemptory move. Grasping him in a neckhold, she forced his head down, burying it between her breasts. Full minutes seemed to pass.

"Don't you think you'd better let him up for air?" I finally asked.

When the girl released him, Tate was breathless, his face flushed, glasses fogged over. "You know," he said, fishing his dollar bill out of his pants pocket, "that wasn't nearly as bad as I thought it would be."

The next morning we were up at 4:30, which is the part I dislike most about waterfowling, and a half hour before dawn we were lying on our backs in a frozen wheat stubble field—the part I dislike second most.

Due to the steady headwind I had managed to miss the first day of goose hunting, which I have to admit is not Sweetzer's or my favorite sport. Evidently it had been an unprecendented PR disaster for our host. The prominent American gun manufacturer that was sponsoring the hunt had presented each of the attending outdoor writers with brand-new automatic shotguns, a model that the company was just preparing to introduce to the public. Because we hook-and-bullet writers are notorious for being easily compromised, in this way the manufacturer expected to get a bunch of cheap publicity. But that morning every one of the guns jammed after the first shot. The deeply embar-

rassed representative from the firearms firm promised to send new guns to all the attending writers after they got home, and clearly heads were going to roll back at the factory.

Now with the first dim light of day came the part I like about goose hunting—a hundred thousand mixed snow geese and Canadas getting up off their evening roost on a nearby lake, a swarm like a single organism, the sound an enormous natural cacophony that has no equal on earth, the rich musical warbles of the birds, the din of thousands upon thousands of beating wings, a sound that has been described as being like that of a freight train or a stadium full of rabid soccer fans, but (to crib from the wonderful writer Terry Tempest Williams) to me sounds like the voice of God. The birds circled in ever-widening arcs, gaining altitude, and it didn't appear that they were going to stop in our stubble field after all. Instead they seemed to line out and we lay on our backs staring up as flock after flock flew over, too high to shoot and impervious to the efforts of expert goose callers in our group. I didn't care; it was a wonder to behold all those birds, flying south on their annual migration just like they always have, year after year, for centuries.

"I've been meaning to ask you, Douglas," I said to my friend, who lay in a blind next to mine. "What will you do with that autoloader they're going to give you?" Tate, who was covering the goose hunt for an English sporting publication, is one of America's foremost experts on British shotguns, author of the excellent book *Birmingham Gunmakers*, and a lover of fine double-barreled shotguns; I just couldn't imagine him shooting, much less owning, an automatic.

Douglas seemed to consider the question. "I don't know," he finally answered, "saw the barrel off and use it to rob convenience stores, I suppose."

Just then one of the writers in our group, no longer able to stand watching the birds fly over just out of range, leaped up from his blind and started shooting at the geese way overhead; you could hear the shot pellets bouncing off their breasts, but

one or two pellets must have hit home with enough energy, for one bird, clearly crippled, began a long gliding descent, coming down in a field a half-mile or so away.

"Someone should go look for that bird," one of the guides said.

"Sweetz and I will go," I quickly volunteered, happy for any opportunity to get up and move around.

But when we got to the approximate place where we had seen the bird down, the cover was thick, almost impenetrable, and though we crisscrossed it for over an hour we could not find the wounded goose. I felt terrible about that and irritated at the man who had taken the "sky-busting" shot.

That night the chamber of commerce of greater Bottineau, North Dakota, the local county seat, invited us all to a Ducks Unlimited dinner banquet to kick off the next day's team goose-hunting competition, in which a number of our party were participating. The high school gymnasium in Bottineau had been festively decorated for the occasion by a committee of the townswomen, and as I wandered about looking at the bad sporting art on the walls ("*A wolf pack is on a hunt. Can you find them?*" asked one trick painting), I overheard a local fellow remark, "What a beautiful job the ladies have done here tonight. Why, they've got this place fixed up prettier than the lobby at the Holiday Inn!" I'm not being cynical or a smart-ass when I say that it's things like this that I love about the north country. Or later when I asked the waitress at our local watering hole in Kramer, the Cork & Bottle, if the chicken on the menu was fried and she gave me that world-weary café waitress look, a look suggesting that I was the most ignorant human being on the face of the earth. "*Everything's* fried, honey," she answered.

After dinner at the banquet, the mayor of Bottineau, who was serving as master of ceremonies of the event, stood up at his place to welcome us to their fair city. He proudly announced

that a number of outdoor writers were in attendance tonight, and would they all please stand up so that everyone could see them. Most of the writers rose somewhat sheepishly (though, seeing the moment coming a mile away, I had made a beeline to the bar and therefore avoided the embarrassment altogether), and one member of the outdoor press, a heavyset and particularly turgid fellow with a bad hairpiece, actually waved to the crowd of appreciative Bottineauvians! Where else in America but the north land can a bunch of hook-and-bullet hacks (and I include myself in that coterie) be looked upon as bona fide celebrities?

It's true that this part of the United States, so far north, is like no other region and that its people, isolated both geographically and psychically from the rest of the nation, are a bit different. Perhaps all that big, flat, often featureless country—country mostly of horizon—has some weird psychological effect on them, that coupled with the nearly constant prairie winds, the remorseless winters, and those roads straight as plumb lines.

After the banquet we went back to the elementary school in Kramer, where we sat around for a while on old sprung couches in the hallway. A young local kid who worked for the outfitter told us a story about the time last spring when he was harrowing his father's wheat fields; he was in a hurry because he was planning to meet some friends at the movies in town, but his father called him on the CB radio and told him that when he was finished harrowing he had to drive the tractor over and leave it at another field. The boy was angry about this, because it meant that he would miss the movie, and he was driving fast down the highway when he noticed a hawk on the road in front of him feeding off roadkill. Like many farmers and ranchers, the boy hated raptors on general principle, simply because, like wolves and coyotes, they are predators. When he saw the hawk, he thought to himself, *I couldn't be so lucky. It'll fly before I hit it.* But for some reason the hawk, intent on its meal, did not fly in time, and when it did it was too late and the boy hit it square

with the grille of the tractor. "There were feathers flying every-where!" the boy recalled happily. "They even came out of the air-conditioning vents inside the cab! I'll tell you, it was worth missing the movie for."

All of which is to say that it is not only urbanites and sub-urbanites who can be removed from the natural world; many rural folks, too, under the guidance of the U.S. Department of Agriculture, the ag colleges, the chemical and farm equipment companies, continue to turn our farmlands, our precious coun-tryside, into factories—unnatural, chemically altered monocul-tures where pests and predators dare not tread, where a young man can take such joy in killing a hawk with a tractor, where dying hamlets tell their own tales of an infrastructure that has betrayed them, where strip mall development on the outskirts of the larger hamlets makes ghost towns of Main Street, and where the cheesy lobby of the Holiday Inn is the final paragon of good taste and might, in a pinch, even serve as a broad meta-phor for the illusory dreams of rural America. So I take it back; there is blame to be laid—all over the place. Just ask the Indians.

The next morning dawned cold and drizzly, and we lay once again in the wheat stubble at first light, staring skyward at the huge flocks of geese winging overhead. Such a timeless spectacle beheld from such a supine position encourages one to take the long view, and it struck me that however much this countryside may have been changed by the activities of man, from way up there things probably didn't look all that much different down here.

That afternoon Doug Tate and I hooked up the Airstream and headed west for Montana, where we had a date to hunt sharp-tails and pheasants. I can't say that either one of us was sorry

to leave. While we can both appreciate the gaudy spectacle, the natural pageantry of the fall goose migration, we're upland hunters in our hearts, walkers, for whom waterfowling tends to be a bit too sedentary. In any case, the true art of goose hunting lies in the calling and decoying, and if you're just along for the ride while the real pros bring the birds in for you the actual shooting is distinctly anticlimactic.

Tate doesn't drive automobiles ("I tried it twice," he says simply when queried on the matter, "and I knew it just wasn't for me"), but he's an excellent navigator, a bright fellow, and fine company. We had both been amused to learn during our visit to this north country that there exists a deep-seated rivalry and competition between eastern Montanans and western North Dakotans—Nodaks, as the latter are disparagingly called—and that the Montanans like to think of themselves as somehow superior to the North Dakotans. There are even jokes about it.

"Jim," said Douglas just as we were crossing the border, "have you heard the story about the Nodak who was so angry with his Montana neighbor that he threw a stick of dynamite over the border?"

"No, I haven't heard that one, Douglas," I answered.

"Yes, well, the Montanan picked it up, lit it, and threw it back."

WINTER

10

ON THE BORDER WITH TATE

Mar. 1876
  *As we halted for the night, a small covey of pin-tailed grouse
flew across the trail. [Gen. George] Crook, with seven shots of
his rifle, laid six of them low, all but one hit in the neck or
head. This shooting was good, considering the rapidity with
which it had to be done, and also the fact that the shooter's
hands were numb from a long march in the saddle and the
cold. These birds figured in an appetizing stew at our next
breakfast.*

  —Capt. John G. Bourke, *On the Border with Crook*

Doug Tate and I were headed first to Westby, Montana, where
we were meeting a fellow named Justin Adams to hunt pheasants and sharptail grouse (or pintail, as they were once familiarly
known). Westby is a tiny town just over the North Dakota
border and just south of the Canadian line. It was late enough
in the season and we were far enough north that the leaves

were off the trees and there was a distinct sense of winter in the air.

We stopped in the local tavern to have a beer when we first pulled into town. It was late afternoon, already dusk, and we were the only customers and we sat up at the bar and chatted with the young man who served us. Behind him, lined up on a shelf, various-sized jars of pickled turkey gizzards, pickled eggs, pickled pig's feet, and pickled calves' brains had the look of formaldehyde-preserved specimens in a high school biology lab.

The young man was amiable and seemed old beyond his years. At the risk of contradicting my earlier remarks about the social and economic failings of modern agriculture, it is also true that some kids who grow up in rural areas, especially on farms and ranches, possess a maturity that is often lacking in urban and suburban kids. Perhaps it has something to do with the fact that they still tend to live closer to the natural cycles of the land—to the rhythms of weather, crops, wildlife, animal husbandry, and the processes of life and death. We asked the young man what the winters were like up in this country. He smiled wryly and said, "That's what everyone always asks us."

"Well?"

"You have no idea," he said, shaking his head. "You can't imagine how cold it gets. Or how boring it is."

The young man had just completed high school and was planning his escape from Westby at the earliest opportunity. It is also a sad fact of rural life that most of the kids can't wait to get off the farm or ranch, away from the stultifying boredom of small town existence, and off to the big city.

We finished our beers, wished the kid good luck, and followed Adams's directions to the mobile home he was renting on the edge of town for several weeks of bird season. Adams had told me over the phone that he would be home late this evening, so we hooked the Airstream up next to his place, set up the grill, and grilled a brace of ducks that we had brought with us from North Dakota.

Douglas Tate, a writer and part-owner of British Game Guns (a Seattle-based company that imports English shotguns), and I had gotten to know each other over the phone, but the trip to North Dakota was the first time we had actually met. I don't often ask people to travel in the Airstream with me, and when I do they are generally close friends, but I had made an exception in Doug's case because, as sometimes happens, I could tell on the phone that we were going to become fast friends. And so we have.

Now we sat at the dining table in the Airstream and ate our ducks, grilled crispy on the outside, rare on the inside, served with wild rice, French bread, and a salad. We drank a bottle of red wine with our dinner. The temperature had fallen fast with the early setting sun, but the Airstream was warm and snug.

Tate told me that he had grown up in a working-class family in the English town of Newcastle upon Tyne, a long way from my own relatively cushy upbringing in the Chicago suburbs. Born in an inner-city tenement, six family members living in two rooms without electricity, he had a hard childhood on the mean streets of Newcastle, where he had to be prepared to defend himself in nearly daily fistfights with neighborhood toughs and even school provided scant refuge from the violence; brutal Dickensian schoolmasters caned, slapped, and punched their unruly charges on the least pretense. It was a drinking man's culture, where fathers and husbands spent much of their free time in the pub and where incidents of spousal and child abuse were so common as to go unremarked upon.

When Douglas was five years old, the socialist government of the day moved his family to a housing project just on the edge of town. The back of his new house looked out over green fields, which change of scenery would have a profound effect on Tate's life. "It would be like a kid from Harlem," he said, "suddenly finding himself in the green hills of New Jersey." Douglas developed an intense interest in bird life and the natural world;

he and his friends went into the fields pretending to be hunters and eventually, in the way of kids, became hunters.

Tate's father was an invalid for most of Douglas's childhood and a reader, so that there were always books around the house, a fact that would prove to be the boy's other avenue to salvation. He lost himself in books, which not only reinforced his love of nature and the outdoors but also offered escape from the grime and violence of daily life in Newcastle.

"I go home once every year or two," Doug told me now as we ate our dinner in the Airstream, "and when I go down to the neighborhood pub all of the same people I grew up with are still there. When I walk in they say, 'Oh, hello, Douglas'; then they go back to their pints. It's as if I never left."

But leave he did, proof of D. H. Lawrence's maxim that "the only true aristocracy is the aristocracy of consciousness." A voracious reader, without benefit of a college education, Tate became a self-taught intellectual, a gourmand, an oenophile, a gentleman, and a sportsman. He had started "rough" shooting in England—mainly rabbits and pigeons—which, given the rigid class system in Great Britain, is all that a working-class boy, forever "branded on the tongue," could hope for. But when he came to the United States a whole continent lay at his feet, as well as a tradition of sporting democracy—a paradise of open country and public access.

The next morning we went hunting with Justin Adams. Adams is an intense, fit, energetic man with intelligent, piercing blue eyes and a kind of clipped, staccato manner of speaking that betrays a military background. He had been a medic in Vietnam and was clearly the sort of fellow you wouldn't mind having around in a tight spot.

Adams had been coming up to the northeast corner of Montana for the past few bird seasons and would stay for several

weeks at a time, buying both Montana and North Dakota hunting licenses, which allowed him to hunt on both sides of the border and kill two limits of birds every day if he felt like it. He was hardly a casual hunter and owned five bird dogs, which he rotated, wearing them all out in the course of a day. But bird populations were down this season, and Adams just wasn't finding the same numbers of pheasants or sharptail grouse as in previous years.

The country hereabouts was hilly, with a number of State Waterfowl Production Areas, wetlands, and prairie potholes full of geese and ducks, flocks of sandhill cranes heading south high overhead, making their deep, warbling crane sounds.

Smart and full of controversial opinions, Adams leaned forward over the steering wheel of his truck as we drove to the hunting grounds and held forth on such subjects as gun control, the Constitution, race, and Bill Clinton, who, like many conservatives, he loathed with a fervor not felt for any other American political figure in this century.

Personally, I'd just as soon have politics left at home on sporting trips. A pretty good argument can be made that one reason we hunt and fish in the first place is that these activities engage us to the extent that we forget for a time such worldly matters. I have, for instance, a number of sporting companions whose politics I don't even know, don't want to; the subject simply never comes up. We live in the moment, and even after the hunt, around cocktails in the Airstream or around a campfire, our interest and conversation seems to be centered on the matters of birds, dogs, shotguns, and the country. But Adams seemed, if not obsessed, at least preoccupied with the generally sorry state of America's morals and politics and social attitudes. I couldn't help but like and admire the guy for his obvious intelligence and convictions, but even as we were hunting he would sidle over and begin a new harangue about some hot-button issue or other. Then he would stop and fix either Douglas

or me with his intense bright blue eyes and demand, "Do you agree with me?" It was clearly not a rhetorical question. We felt like we were being quizzed by a particularly demanding school-master, and after the stories Tate had told the previous evening about his childhood, I rather expected Adams to rap us smartly over the knuckles with a cane if we gave unsatisfactory answers. I really liked the guy, but he made me a bit nervous; he seemed isolated and somehow lonely within the cocoon of his opinions.

We left as planned the next morning, headed for a date to hunt farther south around Glendive, Montana, with yet another group of friends.

So we drove—or I should say I drove and Tate navigated—through Plentywood, Antelope, Medicine Lake, Culbertson, Sidney, Crane, and Savage, following the Yellowstone River south. We talked about books, food, wine, birds, travel, country. Douglas was better-educated by far than I on all such topics, without being in the least bit pedantic, and I loved listening to him talk. He told me that he and his wife, Bonny, who is a professional chef trained at the Cordon Bleu, belong to group of "foodies"—friends who get together regularly to cook and eat and whose interests are every bit as specific, exclusionary, and obsessive as those of bird hunters.

We were meeting three fellows from Idaho in Glendive—Bill Vanderbilt, Patrick McIntyre, and Butch Harper. All three were serious, excellent bird hunters who travel a great deal themselves in the fall, do their homework, study the maps, and keep de-tailed hunting journals with specific information about each re-gion. In new country they hang out in the local cafés, drink coffee, and talk with the residents, trying to glean information about ranchers and farmers in the area who might be willing to let them on their property. The future of bird hunting in the United States seems to be going inexorably the way of Europe, with the privatization and leasing of hunting lands by individ-uals, groups, or clubs or by outfitters who buy up leases and then

charge large fees to guide wealthy sportsmen. It is an inevitable function of both growing human populations on dwindling wildlife habitat as well as the depressing fact that in our culture such relatively arcane wildlife as game birds, and the pursuit thereof, must demonstrate some genuine economic value in order to be allowed to exist.

But these guys did it the old-fashioned way; they knocked on doors, schmoozed with the landowners, got to know something of the locals' lives—their interest perhaps self-serving but nevertheless entirely genuine. Come Christmastime the hunters even send cards and presents to the ranchers and farmers so as not to be forgotten by them from one season to the next.

And they were walkers, these men, which was fine with me and Douglas. There was a certain contour to the prairie around Glendive, the gentle rolling plains cut by coulees, huge good country, and we spread out across it, all of us, the dogs running their particular tangents, with a sense of freedom and common purpose, man and dog alike focused on one object, one goal, the birds flying wild out ahead of us, our pure shared joy at being alive, at walking the miles through the prairies with like-minded friends, the simplicity and rightness of it that has so few parallels in our modern life. Later we would cook birds in the Airstream and on camp stoves in front of Glendive's Budget Host Inn, the hunter-friendly motel where these fellows were staying. We would cook and laugh and eat and drink wine and sit propped up by pillows on the motel beds where our weary dogs slept the deep sleep of hunters. Maybe this, after all, is why we hunt, to reduce our lives to something so elemental and uncomplicated.

Early one morning I drove Doug Tate back over the border to the airport in Minot, North Dakota. I dropped him off and headed back to Montana to pick up the Airstream. Some weather was moving in, and as I crossed the badlands between

North Dakota and Montana at dusk the wind came up, pushing dark gray storm clouds across the barren landscape. A few fat drops of rain the size of silver dollars splattered against the windshield, and then, as if announcing an end to the hunt, it began to pour.

11

STINKING WOMAN CREEK

The earth is all that lasts.

—*Black Elk Speaks*, John Neihardt

We were in southwestern Nebraska, far off the beaten path, up a drainage called Stinking Woman Creek (the details of which name are too revolting to go into, involving as it does a two-week-old Cheyenne Indian woman's corpse and a conspicuously lonely French-Canadian fur trapper). This was the heart of farm country, small river bottom towns, each with its semiabandoned main street—the old defunct hardware store, the five-and-dime, the storefront plate glass windows cracked and final LIQUIDATION SALE signs still visible. Each little town has its grain elevator, the agricultural co-op, the Anhydrous Ammonia company office, its fleet of tank trucks lined up in the parking lot like military vehicles poised for a final assault upon the American countryside.

It was mid-December and pheasant season had been on for over a month. We had come here cold, Mike, Steve, and I,

prospecting new country, but we were having trouble finding a place to hunt today, and the day was stretching on. We had already been turned down several times, or no one had been home where we'd stopped to ask. Small farming and ranching being what it is these days, many of the landowners and their wives had been forced to take jobs in town. Indeed, the history of the family farm was written on the land here like a living museum, telling a sad tale of failed fortunes—from old, crumbling original homestead, to long abandoned farmhouse, to mobile homes, many of these collapsed like a house of cards, abandoned after the farm had been absorbed by a larger concern.

Besides absent owners and being turned down flat or discouraged by leased land postings, we'd also heard today every evasive tactic that farmers use to avoid letting hunters on their property without being downright rude about it. "Well, I can't let you hunt here," said one fellow regretfully, as if it were quite out of his hands, "but you might try asking over to Hoot's place." But when we stopped at Hoot's place we were greeted in the farmyard by an ancient fat, gray-muzzled, half-blind black Lab who barked at us without real conviction, and Hoot wasn't even at home. As we later learned, he was where he is every afternoon— down at the local grain elevator playing poker with the boys.

So then we stopped by Hoot's neighbor's on the other side, the farmyard full of an astonishing variety of junked cars and farm implements, a third-world-looking place, where we found the owner in his shop up to his elbows in grease working on a piece of unidentifiable machinery. "I keep hoping to break even one of these years," he said by way of greeting.

But the "junk man," as we would later refer to him, wouldn't let us hunt, either. "Don't have any birds here anymore, fellas," he told us with a sad shake of his head, another favorite landowner excuse. "You'd be wasting your time. Used to have birds all over the place. Don't know what's happened to 'em. . . . I swear ever since we let a man walk on the moon the birds have been on a steady downswing."

So now Mike, our designated permission asker, stood on the porch of a place that we thought driving in looked sort of promising. They had, for instance, a couple of Brittanies who looked suspiciously like hunting dogs in their fenced yard. But we could see that things were not going well for Mike. The woman to whom he was talking had come out on the porch, a good sign, because it meant that she at least trusted Mike not to be a serial killer, which these days is a start at least, but she kept shaking her head, which was definitely not a good sign. Finally, so much time passed that I decided to get out of the vehicle and see if I couldn't help Mike out. I'm not proud of it, but when all else fails our last-ditch ploy is for Mike to introduce me as a famous outdoor writer.

"Mrs. Stratton, here," said Mike, briefing me on the progress of negotiations so far, "won't allow anyone from Colorado to hunt on her property, because the last time she did the hunters left the gates open and the stock got out." (C'mon, hunters, how hard is it to shut a damn gate? Why make things hard for all of us?)

"Well, you don't have to worry about that with us, ma'am," I assured her. "We always shut our gates."

And then Mike introduced me as a famous outdoor writer. Mrs. Stratton was distinctly unimpressed; she'd clearly heard that one before. In fact, she told us that one time some years ago Gene Hill had hunted here. "What did you say your name was?" she asked me.

So then I asked her about her Brittanies. It turned out that they were from the line of a trainer with whom I was familiar. We made some small inroads on this score, the subject of people's bird dogs being a great icebreaker. Mrs. Stratton actually seemed to be softening. We made further promises to shut all gates; we cajoled; we stopped just short of begging—no, that's not true. . . . We actually begged.

And finally Mrs. Stratton cracked under our relentless double-team assault. She agreed to let us hunt her property and gave

us specific directions on where to start. "Don't go near the sow on the other side of the road," she cautioned. "She'll tear your leg off. And don't shoot my cows."

She paused and looked hard at us. "And, boys," she said sternly. "If you find any birds . . . don't miss!"

So now Sweetz and I were hunting along the wide, winding river bottom of Stinking Woman Creek. Brown fall leaves floated motionless in the slaty greenish-gray water, the yellowed grass matted thick on the banks. Enormous old-growth cottonwoods, bare now of leaves, stood starkly against a flat winter sky.

Steve and his Brittany, Kate, hunted up above us on the edge of a wheat stubble field, and Mike and his Brit, Belle, worked a cornfield on the opposite side of the creek. The fields were relatively small, their size dictated by the undulating, uneven hills of this country, shadowed already by an afternoon sun rushing toward the fall equinox.

Sweetz and I walked up on a hawk carcass dangling from a string; I called her in close, knowing that it was a predator bait and that a steel leghold trap meant to ensnare a coyote, fox, or bobcat lurked somewhere underfoot. It was an eerie scene, the dead hawk suspended so still like that. We moved carefully out of the vicinity.

Sweetz started to get birdy and then suddenly went on point. Yes, I know, she's not a pointing dog, but now and then, especially if she sees a bird on the ground, she will freeze up just like a pointer. A rooster labored out from under a tangle of deadfall as if in slow motion; I could hear his efforts before I could see him, and when he finally appeared and launched himself, flying low to the ground, he presented an easy shot. I missed. Both barrels. Merry Christmas, pheasant.

I climbed up out of the bottom to join Steve on the bench, and Kate pointed a covey of quail on the edge of the wheat stubble and we shot a few birds. A front was blowing in; we could feel in our bones the barometer dropping, the cold wind

moaning through the bony cottonwoods. It was winter now for sure.

Mike and Steve were heading back to Colorado in the morning, and I was headed in my own direction, as yet undetermined. We ate dinner in the Airstream, which was camped out front of the motel where they were staying. The Soo-Paw, it was called, for Sioux-Pawnee, and pretty much all that is left hereabouts of those tribes. A typical plains motel, circa 1960s— oddly festive with Christmas decorations already up outside and tinny carols playing on the lobby speakers. For dinner I roasted three sharptail grouse that I'd brought with me from Montana— stuffed with sautéed garlic, chopped gizzards, green onions, and green grapes, a sauce made from game stock and pan drippings, served with braised leeks and roast tomatoes, thinly sliced *pommes frites*, a vinaigrette salad, a baguette, and a nice bottle of Margaux.

Sweetz lay exhausted on the bed, her eyes leaking fluid and her nose bloody from busting brush and plowing through heavy grass all day. She was too tired even to get up and beg, which for a Lab is really tired. She seemed old to me tonight, the first time I'd really noticed.

As we were finishing dinner a blast of arctic wind rocked the Airstream and Steve and Mike and I looked at one another and smiled; we knew we were in for it. But right now we were snug and sated and content. There are certain moments in this sporting life that we remember for the rest of our lives, and this would be one of them—preceded by a hard day's hunt, a few birds in the bag, and followed by a winter storm blowing in, this dinner was etched already in our collective hunter's memory, as if in a photo album of Christmases past.

It was bitterly cold and there was a skiff of swirling snow on the ground in the morning when Mike and Steve knocked on the

door to say good-bye. We shook hands and patted one another on the shoulder, promising another hunt another day, sorry to be parting, for we were friends and hunters. I watched them sadly as they drove away from the Soo-Paw Motel, the colored Christmas lights along the roofline still burning cheerfully in the faint light of dawn.

12

SPIRITS RUNNING

Sweetz and I were camped out in the Airstream at Nebraska's Fort Robinson, now a State Park and museum. It was off-season at the park, winter, and we were the only campers in the campground. I liked the country—the sandy pine-studded bluffs behind the green perfectly manicured grounds of the old fort; the white barracks and cottage-style officers' houses all lined up with perfect military precision; the densely treed river bottoms in which deer and wild turkeys abound.

At the same time it is a lonely, melancholy place—you can feel the ghosts and spirits abroad, and the ground here is soaked in blood. It was here, in 1877, that the great Sioux chief Crazy Horse was murdered. And it was here, on a clear, frigid January night in 1879, with the moon full and the temperature well below zero and a fresh cover of snow on the ground, that 149 Cheyenne men, women, and children broke out of a locked barracks, climbing one by one through a tiny window. They overpowered the guards and ran across this campground, right

past where I was now camped, trying to escape into the river bottom below.

Roused out of bed by the cries of their fellows, the soldiers organized quickly and hunted the fleeing Cheyennes down. Those Indians who were not killed or recaptured that first night and who refused to surrender died a few days later in a cave on a nearby bluff when the soldiers emptied their rifles into the cave until a terrible silence prevailed. When the smoke cleared and the soldiers entered the cave, they found the Cheyenne bodies stacked like Holocaust victims, which in a genuine sense they were—the men lying atop the women, the women covering their children. I wanted to go see that cave, which is on private property outside the fort grounds, but it is, quite rightly, a secret and a sacred place to the Cheyenne and non–tribal members are not allowed there.

And you may choose to believe that I dreamed this part if you like, and maybe I did—maybe it is simply our dreams that conjure ghosts—but late that first night at Fort Robinson, as I lay in bed in the Airstream with Sweetz curled next to me, she suddenly jerked awake, the hackles rising on her back, a low growl issuing from her throat. A cold tingle ran up my spine, and I swear that I heard the muffled sounds of running feet outside and faint, nearly inaudible cries and whispers that were not in a language I knew. The Cheyennes believe that everything that ever happens in a place still resides there, so that the past, present, and future live on forever in the earth.

The next morning—the last day of pheasant season—dawned clear and cold. Sweetz and I left the Airstream with gun in hand and dog bell on collar. The cottonwoods were bare, the heavy fall grasses whorled on the ground, covered with a sheen of frost. We hunted the edge of cover along the river and flushed three pheasants in a row, all of them hens. We hunted along an old railroad bed, Sweetz putting her head down and bulling her way through dense, tangled thickets, quartering back and forth across

a half-collapsed barb wire fence that followed the tracks. She rooted out three more hens, one after the next. Each time I mounted my gun and swung on the bird, but, of course, because it was a hen, I did not shoot. Sweetz didn't seem to mind. It wasn't until we had circled back to the Airstream for lunch that I noticed the blood on her chest and, on closer examination saw the jagged six-inch barbwire gash, her hide laid open to reveal the marbled muscle beneath.

The local vet in nearby Crawford was working a cattle sale barn that afternoon, and so I drove the thirty or so miles to the Animal Care Clinic in Chadron, Nebraska. There veterinarian Colleen Mitchell stitched Sweetz up while her assistant, Joli, and I held her down. As intrepid and fearless as she is in the field, Sweetz is an enormous baby when it comes to going to the doctor; though under local anesthetic, she squirmed and whined and generally embarrassed me in front of these very competent women.

After better than an hour spent patching Sweetz up, Dr. Mitchell presented me with the bill—a whopping twenty-six dollars.

"The stitches can come out in about ten days," she instructed. "In the meantime, keep her out of the water."

"Yeah, right," I said. "Try keeping a hunting Lab out of the water for ten days."

"Well, you might just have to quit hunting for a while," she said.

"I never thought of that," I answered.

So Sweetz—a prominent row of stitches across her shaved chest—and I got back to the Airstream at dusk. The weather forecast called for bitter cold tonight, and already I could feel the temperature dropping. And I felt an acute pang of loneliness, a sense of the heartbreak that permeated this bloody ground. I wondered if tonight we would hear again the sounds of those desperate human beings fleeing in the snow. I knew that in my

dreams the Cheyennes would still be out there—the unsettled ghosts of the men, women, and children running eternally for the river, running for their lives.

Just as we were about to enter the trailer I heard the distinctive *whoosh* of wings cutting the air. Sweetz and I both stopped and looked up in astonishment as three cock pheasants sailed directly over the Airstream; wings set, they glided past like apparitions, landing soundlessly in a fencerow not fifty yards away. We watched the birds down.

13

MOUNTAIN MAN

Like me, mountain man Dean Wavrunek brings along his own lodging when he travels—and by that I mean, literally, a lodge—constructed of true lodgepole pines and a canvas covering painted with symbolic figures. He hauls the poles behind his pickup on a custom-built trailer—the modern equivalent of a travois—and when he finds a good place to camp it takes him a couple of hours to set up, lashing the poles together and stretching the canvas across them. The last thing he does is hang a painted buffalo skull with various totems dangling off it from a scalp pole in front of the entrance and then build a fire in the center of his lodge. I must say it makes my Airstream with its propane furnace and other amenities seem kind of vulgar.

We were both camped out behind a goose-hunting camp in Minnesota. Although I consider myself to be somewhat of a student of Native American cultures, I was not exactly certain of the protocol for entering another man's tepee in the late twentieth century. I mean it's not like the mountain man had a smiley sign hanging on the door the way that friendly folks

do in RV parks—a signal that one is receiving visitors. My Indian books suggest that you simply scratch lightly on the covering at the lodge entrance, which I did while at the same time checking out the scalp pole, wondering as I did so, *Just how authentic is this guy?*

Actually, Wavrunek is, by vocation, the sheriff of the tiny town of Verdigre, Nebraska. He is a mountain man as a kind of avocation. He wears a large mustache and a hairstyle reminiscent of Buffalo Bill. Wavrunek and his wife make all their own clothes, and they eat whatever they can hunt, as well as assorted roadkill. When on the very rare occasion that Dean is forced to dine in a restaurant the first thing he always asks the waitress is, "You got any wild critters on the menu?" And he will not, under any circumstances, eat pork. "I won't eat no pig meat," he says disdainfully one morning in the lodge as a platter of bacon is passed around the breakfast table. He shakes his head darkly. "That pig meat ain't no good for you."

On general mountain man principle, Wavrunek will only hunt with a flintlock rifle that he made himself (a replica of a model manufactured in the 1830s by Jacob and Melchoir Fordney) or with a bow and arrow (a Nez Percé friend is currently making him an authentic Indian bow, for which he will make his own arrows). Modern rifles and even percussion guns simply do not present enough of a shooting challenge to Wavrunek anymore, nor do they own the same kind of romance that is attached to his beloved flintlock.

However, in this case romance had come up against hard modern reality and Wavrunek was faced with a bit of a dilemma—the next morning we were going out to the cornfields to hunt geese, and Dean had already requested and been denied permission by the local wildlife officer to shoot lead shot in his flintlock. So that evening Dean cut open a couple of twenty-gauge shells and salvaged the steel shot and plastic shot cup. Though he was loathe to shoot plastic (or, for that matter, steel)

through his flintlock, pursuing the mountain man life these days requires a certain amount of compromise and adaptability.

Dean Wavrunek is an example of one of the things that I like best about the sporting community—and that is its broad diversity of individuals, interests, styles, and talents. If the hunter who chooses to shoot waterfowl with an autoloader and three-inch Magnum shells can be said to represent one end of the spectrum, Wavrunek stakes out the other end, and there is plenty of room in between for all the rest of us. Besides being a consummate outdoorsman and an accomplished craftsman, he is also a master tomahawk thrower—yet another outdoor skill that has fallen into some disregard in this century. So the next time you make what you consider to be a really good shot with a rifle or shotgun, consider that the mountain man can do this: In shooting demonstrations at various events, he plants a double-bitted ax on a board with the other blade facing out. He hangs two blue stones attached to strips of rawhide on either side of the blade. He paces off, steadily aims his flintlock, fires. The musket ball flies straight and true, lands dead-center on the blade of the ax, splitting like an atom in two perfect halves, each of which shatters one of the stones on either side of the ax blade.

That night in the lodge I got talking to Dean about his mountain man philosophy. He told me how as a boy he was always fascinated by Daniel Boone and Davy Crockett, and how one year he asked Santa for a Davy Crockett outfit for Christmas and that was the beginning of his life as a mountain man. He explained that he was not in the least bit interested in national or international politics. "I don't give a damn what's happening in the rest of the world," he said, "because it don't have any real effect on my life. I only care about what happens in my own town." So Dean is kind of the ultimate localist; neither a passenger on the information highway nor in the least bit interested in politics or current events or international affairs, he

is a throwback to another, simpler time. However deeply eccentric and even impractical this may seem, it's a fine notion anyway, and one can't help but marvel at the rare man who practices it.

The next morning just past dawn we were lying prone in the corn stubble, concealed beneath cornstalks. We had agreed that Dean would take the first shot, but with the limited range of his flintlock, he explained, that he wouldn't risk shooting unless the caller could bring the geese into the decoys within twenty-five yards or so of where we lay. Clearly one learns to take only killing shots with antique weaponry—a discipline from which all hunters might benefit.

We had a couple of world-class callers in our group, and they turned the first goose that came in over the cornfield. The cold dawn sky was streaked in fading pink and the air was beginning to fill with the distant honking of incoming geese, like cracked pepper on the horizon. The lone goose turned, circled, looked us over, and circled again, losing altitude, finally setting his wings over the decoys and coming in for a soft landing. Now Dean sat up, popping out from under his cornstalks like a scarecrow. He took measured aim, leveling his long gun: *paaah-whuuuumf* spoke the flintlock in two distinct syllables, the wonderful deep, muffled language of sparking flint and igniting powder that brought back something of the frontier in our subliminal hunters' memory. The goose folded. We cheered the mountain man.

14

THE CHRISTMAS GOOSE

We were drifting across the high plains of southeastern Wyoming, returning from a late-December hunt, trying to get home in time for Christmas. I say "drifting" because that's how it felt with the infamous Wyoming wind blowing fingers of snow across the road before us—the bleakest stretch of winter road you can imagine on Christmas Eve. It was just dusk and the light was gray and grainy with the blowing snow, and the Airstream shimmied and slipped on the wind while the Suburban strained mightily to hold things together. We seemed to be the only people abroad this evening, possibly the only people in the universe from the feel of things. I say "we" and "people," but it was just me and Sweetz and Patsy Kline, who was presently singing, *"Crazy . . . I'm crazy for feeling so lonely,"* on the tape deck.

We had made a successful duck and goose hunt along the Platte River in Nebraska, with perfect waterfowling weather—cold and wet and snowy so that the mallards came pitching in waves out of the close dark clouds, wheeling and diving into the

decoys, and the geese began arriving just before dawn in the cut cornfields, their plaintive honking and heavy wingbeats filling the pearly winter skies. It is a paradise out there, this outdoor world, a miracle of wonders.

Now I was only a few hours from home, but with the storm gathering and visibility decreasing steadily I seriously considered pulling off the road and spending the night, which is one of the best features about traveling with one's own accommodations. But it was, after all, Christmas Eve, and I was expected home; I had a fresh Christmas goose in the back of the Suburban, and in any case, if I pulled off now and the snow and wind kept up all night I might never get under way again. Buried alive . . . they'd find me and Sweetz in the spring when the snow drifts thawed enough to reveal a glint of aluminum from our Airstream tomb. . . .

These were the dark thoughts going through my mind this stormy Christmas Eve when suddenly the figure of a man seemed to materialize out of the blowing snow. I thought for a moment that it must be a trick of the dusky evening light and the blowing snow, but as I passed him standing on the side of the road I could clearly make out a large, hulking figure, ill-dressed for the inclement weather and looking unspeakably forlorn.

I will admit that I don't often stop for hitchhikers anymore, given the current climate of murder and mayhem on America's highways and biways. Now I was wondering who could conceivably be hitchhiking way out here on such a winter night? There was a state penitentiary outside Rawlins, not too far away. . . .

But it was Christmas Eve, and you'd have to be a harder man than I to leave someone out in a storm at nightfall in the middle of the Wyoming plains, and so I slowed carefully and came to a halt on the side of the road and put my flashers on in case of approaching traffic; in fact, I hoped for approaching traffic.

I watched the man trotting stiffly toward me; he moved with a vaguely familiar stride and appeared to be carrying a small gas

can in one hand, which made me feel a bit less uneasy. The man came to the passenger side, opened the door, and slipped in, breathing heavily and blowing plumes of steam inside the truck. I was equal parts enormously relieved and completely flabbergasted to see that I knew this fellow; it was my old friend Jack Higginbotham, Higgy we called him, a childhood pal with whom I had had a falling out a few years back over a gundog. I was particularly shocked to see Higgy here because I'd heard that he was dead.

The last time anyone of us had seen Higgy was several years ago. It was around Christmas then, too, and a couple of goons from the city came up to the small town in Wyoming where Higgy was living at the time and were attempting to repossess his truck. Evidently Higgy had apprehended them in the process, for he was hanging onto the driver's side door rain gutter, skating down the snow-packed Main Street as the repo men drove off in his truck. They drove right out of town, Higgy hanging onto the side of his truck for dear life. And no one had seen him or his truck since. Although Higgy was notorious for vanishing for months, even years, at a time, this time, after a while, we all assumed that he was dead, that the repo men had murdered him and stashed his body somewhere out in the plains. Higgy had gotten himself in a good bit of trouble over the past few years. Eventually rumors surfaced that Higgy had been spotted in Mexico, living with a woman named Esperanza, but I had never really believed these.

Now he turned to me and smiled; it made my blood run cold. "Hey, Jimmy," he said as if there were nothing at all odd about running into each other out here in the middle of the Wyoming plains on Christmas Eve after all this time.

"Hey, Higgy," I answered. "I thought you were dead."

He made a dismissive gesture. "As so-and-so said, reports of my death have been greatly exaggerated."

"So you're not dead, right?" I asked, not entirely convinced.

"Do I look dead, Jimmy?" Higgy asked.

"Well, actually, you kind of do, Higgy," I said. Higgy was deathly pale and looked older that I remembered him, and his hair had turned snow white. "What the hell are you doing way out here, anyway?" I asked.

"I was on my way to spend Christmas with some friends, and I ran out of gas a couple of miles up the road," Higgy answered. "I walked all the way back to the last gas station and was headed back to my truck when the storm blew in. But I'm sure glad that you came along when you did, Jimmy. It's getting cold out there."

"What friends?" I asked. "Where?" Higgy was always exhausting his old friendships and making new ones, rehabilitating and reinventing himself in the process.

"Oh, you don't know them," he said. "New friends. I'm on my way there now. Where are you coming from?"

I told him and I described a little of the hunt.

"Boy, that sounds great," Higgy said a bit wistfully. "I haven't hunted in a long time . . . not since the last time you and I went out for sage grouse."

"I remember," I said. "That was a long time ago, wasn't it, Higgy?"

And then it got real quiet inside the truck for a while as Higgy and I both awkwardly recalled our falling out, things that had been said and could never be taken back. Finally, I said, "Maybe you'd like to take a goose to your friends' house for Christmas, Higgy. I've got an extra one in the back."

"That would be great," Higgy replied. "I hate to show up empty-handed on Christmas Eve. A goose would be a nice thing to bring."

A couple of miles down the road we came upon Higgy's truck, which seemed itself to materialize suddenly out of the storm. I was surprised to see that it was the same candy-apple red truck in which the repo men had tried to drive off. Higgy was like a cat with nine lives. I pulled over and stopped behind it, and I got a goose out of the back of the Suburban while Higgy put

the gas in his tank. The snow was coming harder now, blowing horizontal.

"Well, I guess we'd better be off before the storm gets any worse!" Higgy called against the wind.

"Yeah, I guess so!" I yelled back. I laid the goose in the bed of his pickup.

"Thanks for the goose, Jimmy," Higgy said. "Merry Christmas."

"Merry Christmas, Higgy."

15

A CLOSE CALL WITH THE DOG COPS

I was home from my travels for a time and I don't know what got into me, but for one reason or another I decided that my wife and I needed some urban influence in our lives. I will be the first to admit that I am a hopeless country bumpkin—a rube, a hayseed, a hick, a yokel—I've hated cities all my life and have gone to some extraordinary lengths to avoid them.

But I think it was the Spanish poet Lorca who said something to the effect that the well-rounded man must at some point cover himself in the "red dust" of the city—air pollution, I guess—and so I shook the cow manure off my boots and off we went to live in an apartment in town. Of course I go nowhere without Sweetz, but we had been assured that dogs were welcome in this particular building.

Sweetz and I were homesick right off for the Big Open, but we made the best of things, taking long walks every afternoon in the city park. Like many American cities these days, this one had a "goose problem"—hundreds, thousands of Canada geese

had taken up residence in the city parks and on the golf courses. Ironically, one of the great success stories of modern wildlife management—the restoration of goose populations—has become a kind of urban nightmare. Now there were too many geese; the park and golf courses looked like a scene from Alfred Hitchcock's *The Birds*. There were geese everywhere, there was goose poop everywhere, and the birds themselves were a sorry, half-domesticated version of their former wild selves. They spent a lot of time loafing around the scummy city ponds and generally making a nuisance of themselves. They didn't even migrate south anymore. Every now and then they'd just fly over to the nearest golf course to eat some fertilized/herbicized golf course grass.

Of course, to a hunter the obvious solution would be to allow some kind of controlled goose hunting on the golf courses, maybe even on special days in the park (Hunters Day!), but it goes without saying that such a concept will never fly in urban America, and so instead the recreation department of this city spends many thousands of dollars every year trying to trap the excess geese and transplant them to places where they can be legally hunted. However, having by then grown accustomed to easy city living and the amenities it offers, most of these urban geese simply fly back to town at the first opportunity.

So Sweetz and I took long walks every afternoon in the city park. I often took her off the leash because she is quite capable of walking at heel without it, and sometimes I would throw a tennis ball for her to retrieve. Every now and then I even let her make a rush, a kind of playful feint, at the park geese. With no natural predators in the city, I thought it might help keep them on their toes, and she never actually nailed any.

One day early on, another man in the park walking his dog, a terrier, stopped me. I don't know how he knew we weren't from around there, but he obviously did. I may as well have had a sign taped to my forehead: COUNTRY BUMPKIN. KICK ME.

"It's none of my business," the fellow said, "but you know the dog police will give you a ticket for letting your dog off the leash."

"The dog police?" I answered, "But she's not bothering anyone; she's right at heel."

"That doesn't matter," he said. "It's a seventy-dollar fine if they catch you with your dog off the leash."

"What do these dog cops look like?" I asked.

"They drive around in recreation department vans," the man said, "and most of them are mean little bastards who love to write tickets."

That same day in the park I saw a woman throwing a ball for her young Lab to retrieve. I approached her. "Aren't you afraid of getting busted by the dog cops?" I asked.

"Oh, I get busted all the time," she said. "I get at least one ticket a month. But this dog is six months old and he needs to run, and so I just consider it a basic pet expense—like going to the vet."

I hadn't actually seen the dog police yet, but now I was getting paranoid. I still let Sweetz off the leash, but I spent a lot of time looking over my shoulder. And I started hearing more and more dog cop horror stories from my city friends and acquaintances.

One evening after work, Dave Williams, for instance, who owns a brace of well-trained English springer spaniel hunting dogs, took them to his tiny neighborhood park. The park had a small pond; it was late in the day, nearly dusk, and no else was there. Dave looked around, thought the coast was clear, unhooked his dogs from their leashes, tossed a couple of retriever dummies into the water, and sent his dogs for them. All the while the dog police had been watching him through binoculars from their van, and by the time his dogs had retrieved their dummies to hand Dave was being written up for, not one, but two tickets, seventy dollars apiece—one for each leashless dog.

And one day, the dog police came right to my friend Bob

Stanley's door. Evidently someone in his neighborhood had complained about Bob's dogs' barking, and now a dog cop stood at his door demanding to see the vaccination and registration papers for his dogs.

"I hope you told him to kiss your ass," I said, outraged when Bob told me this story. "Did you ask him if he had a search warrant?"

"No, I didn't," Bob said with resignation. "Jim, the guy was packing."

"The dog cop had a gun?"

"Yeah, and of course, my resignation papers weren't exactly in order," Bob said. "By the time it was over it cost me almost three hundred bucks."

Now I was really getting paranoid. I started having nightmares about the dog Gestapo knocking on my door in the middle of the night, demanding to see Sweetzer's city registration papers, which, it goes without saying, we do not have, and so they drag her away, howling, to languish in a sunless cell in dog prison. . . .

And then one day it happened. Sweetz was off the leash in the park; we weren't bothering anyone, she was perfectly under control, she wasn't even chasing the geese, she was just retrieving a tennis ball that I had thrown in order to give her a little exercise, when the dog cops pulled up in their van, two of them descending from either side. They were small, stocky, swarthy fellows in uniforms that included black boots, and one had his ticket pad out and neither of them looked one bit friendly.

By now Sweetz was back at heel, but she didn't like the aggressive way in which the dog cops were approaching us and she started growling at them.

"Bad idea!" I whispered to her. "Knock it off!"

"Your dog is off the leash," the dog cop said. "I'm going to have to write you up."

"Yeah, OK," I said. I didn't want any trouble.

"I need some identification," he said. "I don't see a tag on your dog's collar."

"She's a hunting dog," I said. "She doesn't wear tags; they tend to get hung up when she goes through fences."

"I need proof of city registration," he said.

"I haven't got it," I said. "We're not from around here." Which wasn't completely untrue.

"Then I need to see your driver's license, sir," said the dog cop.

"I don't have my driver's license. I didn't bring my wallet. We're just taking a walk in the park."

"In that case, I'm going to have to impound the dog," he said. "Until you can provide some identification."

"Yeah, right," I said defiantly, "you and six other little guys just like you." It was my worst urban nightmare come true.

"Ramon, get the noose on that dog," the dog cop said to his partner. Clearly, he wasn't fooling around.

But before Ramon could do so, I hollered, "Run, Sweetz!" And the two of us took off across the park, running for our lives.

Ramon pursued us on foot, while the head dog cop—I never did learn his name—jumped in the van. I heard a siren start up. I glanced back over my shoulder to see Ramon speaking into a walkie-talkie as he ran. This cost him valuable time, while Sweetz and I, both of us in tiptop hunting condition, sprinted ahead.

We kept to the middle of the park where the van couldn't follow and there were lots of other people. Other park recreators turned to watch us impassively as we fled, as urbanites will do, and a few dog walkers even shouted words of encouragement as we passed, because everyone hates the dog cops.

Sweetz and I have been in some tough spots before. We've faced giant swamp rats in Alabama, alligators in Florida; we've had close encounters with bears in Colorado, rattlers in Idaho; we've been lost in the wilds of Wisconsin and headwalled on a cliff in Utah. But this was the first time we'd ever been fugitives from the law.

At last we managed to elude the dog cops, losing Ramon in

an alley and making our way back home, where we triple-locked the door of the apartment. For the next few days we only went out at night, and of course we stayed away from the park. Even so, I wore dark glasses and a hat when we ventured forth and Sweetz assumed her shar-pei disguise. (Many Lab owners have discovered that if you take hold of your dog's head with both hands and kind of bunch the skin up and pull it forward, it will be a dead ringer for the wrinkled Chinese breed. A little surgical tape to hold things in place, and voilà!)

Finally we decided that the city was no place for a hunter and a hunter's dog. Under cover of night, we loaded up the Airstream and headed back to the open country.

16

ON CUTTING THE PRESIDENT'S TRAIL

I did not have sexual relations with that woman.

—Pres. Bill Clinton

It was clearly time to introduce some sunlight into our winter environment—the short, cold, dark days of the north were beginning to wear on me and Sweetz. We were headed south, hauling the Airstream down the road near Albuquerque, New Mexico. My friend Jon Williams rode shotgun and two other friends, Dave Christian (D. C.) and Steve Collector, brought up the rear in D. C.'s battered faded-red Toyota Land Cruiser—we formed a short motley caravan of unassuming middle-class American sportsmen, on our way to Arizona to hunt quail.

True to D. C.'s belief that all adventures begin not when you arrive at your destination but as soon as you leave your driveway, we passed an exit cordoned off by a number of police cars with flashing lights. There were vehicles pulled over along the side of the road and sundry officials, uniformed and not, wandering importantly about while yakking into walkie-talkies and cellular

phones. Maybe it's the times we live in or the simple fact that we'd all watched too much television in our lives, but later in comparing notes we learned that we each had the same initial impression of this scene: It was: (1) a drug bust; (2) a shootout; (3) a Bureau of Alcohol, Tobacco, and Firearms showdown with a patriot group and/or fringe religious cult; or (4) all of the above.

A mile or so farther down the road a spanking new Bronco containing four clean-cut, serious-looking fellows in dark suits and sunglasses pulled up alongside us and held even for a few moments while they looked us over and the driver spoke into a car phone. Then they sped forward, cutting dangerously across our front end and onto the shoulder, where they came to an abrupt halt. "What was that all about?" Williams and I wondered out loud, at which point we spotted a long, evenly spaced line of cars with their lights on, headed toward us on the other side of the highway. Now we were thinking that the roadblock and all the related vehicular fanfare must be for the funeral of a particularly important local personage. Until we noticed that the procession was not led by a hearse; rather, it appeared to be a motorcade, the centerpiece of which was a big, shiny black limousine flying an American flag. Well now we were speculating wildly about what dignitary might be riding in that limo when we saw the banner on a hillside across the road. It said: WELCOME PRES. CLINTON. But by then we had just passed the limo and it was too late for me to satisfy the sudden childlike urge I had to wave to the president of the United States.

Turning the radio to a local station, we learned that Bill Clinton was indeed in town for one of those obligatory fifteen-minute visits to an Indian reservation (after which the Indians could be safely ignored for the rest of his term) and then it occurred to us that the suits in the Bronco who had checked us out must have been Secret Service agents, concerned that the Airstream might be carrying explosives or a hit team of Arab terrorists. As a matter of fact, we were well armed back there

(with shotguns, of course), and I've been wondering ever since what means they had at their disposal to learn so quickly our identities and the fact that we were quite harmless. Perhaps Big Brother really is watching us.

Which, believe it or not, brings me to my point. One of the first things you can't help but notice when you happen upon the president of the United States in real life is something you rarely notice when you see him on the evening news—that is, the sheer gauze of unreality through which he is forced to view the world. Insulated by his motorcade and his entourage of aides and protectors, chased everywhere he goes by the relentless, heel-nipping Washington press corps, buffeted this way and that by the ever-changing winds of prevailing public sentiment, transported hither and yon from one carefully choreographed appearance to another—I mean, how is this man supposed to keep any kind of grip at all on reality?

Well, I'll tell you how; and while it's not at all a novel or an earth-shattering idea, it is a very simple one. He needs to get outdoors. And, of course, I'm not talking about a daily run around the White House track or a round of golf to schmooze with some senators or a walk in the woods at Camp David sur-rounded by thirty of his closest advisers or a stroll down the beach at a New Age Renaissance weekend in Hilton Head or a two-hour duck hunt at dawn (staged more to make a political point than to shoot ducks, though better that than, say, brunch in the Rose Garden with Wayne Pacelle).

No, I'm talking Outdoors with a capital O in the sense of an Outward Bound survival experience—all alone, with just his own self and Mother Earth and maybe a length of fishing line and a hook. Outdoors in the way that Teddy Roosevelt once went afield on month-long hunting expeditions into the heart of the American wilderness. Even Outdoors in the considerably more modest way that I and my friends and most of the rest of us enter and experience the natural world—alone or with loved ones and cronies at our sides or maybe just with a beloved dog

at our heels and a shotgun in the crook of our arm or carrying a fishing rod or simply wandering about with a pair of binoculars and a topo map in hand.

Sure, I know that Bill Clinton can't do these things, even if he wanted to—which, sadly, he apparently doesn't. Indeed, TR was the last of the great president-outdoorsmen, the last to be allowed to wander about more or less freely in the wilderness. And I think that's too damn bad, both for President Clinton and for the country. In fact, I believe that such excursions into the outdoors should be mandatory for American presidents, for all politicians for that matter, in the same way that the great native American chiefs Crazy Horse of the Sioux and Little Wolf of the Cheyennes were expected to periodically go up and sit atop a hill for two or three days without shelter or provisions, just to think things over, to seek a vision. God knows our politicians could use some vision, and such periods of reflection and renewal might not only offer some respite from their thankless jobs but also give them some sense of perspective, even honor. It might make them begin to understand what's really important in this world, might make them reflect upon the things that are worth saving, worth fighting for, might help them to take a stand for an actual earth that must seem only an abstraction to them. To be sure, such epiphanies on the part of our elected officials are a great deal to hope for, but one thing for sure—they're not going to happen at thirty thousand feet or from behind tinted windows in the backseat of a bullet-proof limousine.

17

APACHE COUNTRY

A portion of our route today abounded with the partridges
(Gambel's quail) peculiar to this country—never were partridges
so numerous as in this—in the distance of half a mile we must
have seen today from 800 to 1,000.
   —the journals of Henry Smith Turner (October 28, 1848,
      describing a U.S. Army expedition down the Gila River
      near the present-day San Carlos Apache Reservation)

We were already hoping that this wasn't turning into one of those
"you-should-have-been-here-last-year" (or, worse, last century)
sporting trips. We had arrived earlier that day on the 1.8-million-
acre San Carlos Apache Reservation (where the wily Geronimo
was relocated after his first surrender) to hunt desert quail in a
once wild and magnificent land. Our hosts were gunsmith and
instinctive shooting instructor Bill Dowtin from Tucson and his
neighbor Rick Hopkins, a dog trainer and well-known Arizona
field trialer. Both had been hunting the rez for several seasons
now, and all summer on the phone Dowtin had been baiting

me with tales of enormous coveys of 250, 300, 500 Gambel's quail, everyone shooting their limits in a matter of a couple of hours. The biggest problem, evidently, was how to entertain oneself around camp for the remainder of the day, which has never struck me as a major problem. But now suddenly, in the first hunting spot of the day, Hopkins's secret honeyhole on a broad dryland flat, there appeared to be no birds; even worse, the land was so badly overgrazed that there was no cover to hold birds. Plenty of cows, though—horned, half-feral, untended beasts that the federal government, in the infinite hypocrisy and cynicism of the Indian reservation system, dumps onto the reservation in far greater numbers than the land can support. The cattle chew and trample the land down until in some areas it resembles a moonscape and then often die anyway of starvation, disease, and neglect, their carcasses left where they fall; they dot the countryside—carrion on the hoof, expensive vulture bait. It's true that, historically, the Apaches have never really expressed much interest in raising cattle.

Now back at the trucks after our first birdless foray through this bovine wasteland, Rick Hopkins, his two fine German shorthairs lapping thirstily at their water bowl, looked out over his former honeyhole and shook his head. "It breaks my heart to see it like this," he said softly.

Our camp ground is excellent; possessing, as usual, rich grama-grass, and large cedar trees for fuel and shelter. Game is abundant. A black-tailed deer and many partridges (Gambel's quail) were killed today. The latter have been seen in great numbers. Upon their heads are tufted plumes, like those of the California partridges (California quail). Tracks of deer, antelope, bears, and turkeys are numerous. Hares and rabbits are frequently started from their hiding places upon our trail.

—Lt. A. W. Whipple (army expedition through Arizona, January 1854)

We circled the wagons—the Airstream and other vehicles and tents—in a grove of live oak trees down off the road; it was a beautiful, parklike setting despite the ubiquitous cattle sign and the empty quart bottles of malt liquor, neither of which we would allow to discourage us.

We were seven in number, as diverse a group as could meet out here in the desert. Besides Dowtin and Hopkins, there were Steve Collector, contractor Dave Christian, artist Doug Baer, and "dancing sportsman" Jon Williams, who teaches etiquette and ballroom dance to school children around the country. We represented a broad political spectrum, as well, from constitutionalist Dowtin to liberal urbanite Williams. It's true that such mixes can be volatile, and as no one of our party knew everyone else, there was no predicting the alchemy of the company—which is always a mysterious process and which can quickly make or break a hunting trip. Later on, although we couldn't exactly say why and although the hunting itself was only middling, some of us would remember this as one of our best trips.

And don't worry, this won't be another birdless story, because that very first afternoon Williams and I were hunting a hillside above a cattle watering hole when we pushed our first covey of Gambel's quail up into a rocky bowl. Hard on pointing dogs, Gambel's are notorious runners, especially when there is no cover for the birds to hide behind. With the exception of a patch of cholla cacti jungle, and scattered prickly pear—plants quite unpalatable even to the most ravenous cattle—the hillside was rocky and bare, grazed down to dust by the cows that ran wildly before us.

We had only Sweetz with us, Hopkins and his pointers hunting elsewhere that afternoon, and she managed to herd the covey into the bowl, where they had no choice but to fly. Although I try, for obvious reasons, to avoid offering anything that might smack of "expert" advice about any aspect of upland bird hunting, let me just say that while Labs are not exactly the dog of choice for southwestern quail hunting, under certain circum-

stances flushing dogs can be quite effective with running birds. For her part, Sweetz will chase them on the ground until she forces them to fly, which hopefully breaks up and scatters the covey. Then the pointers can hunt the singles, which are far more likely to hold. So Sweetz busted the covey and they spread out across the hillside and we had a couple of hours of interesting shooting, chasing singles back and forth, up and down. Gambel's seem to have their own unique flight patterns—they rarely fly "true"—describing odd angles and trajectories. This, along with the difficult footing offered by the abundant volcanic rock (called malpai—"bad country"), made for challenging shooting.

At one point, true to his nickname, the "dancing sportsman" swung on a bird flying overhead, lost his balance, teetered precariously, took a series of quick balletic steps across the rocks, recovered his balance, still swinging, then teetered again, repeating the same fancy footwork; he reminded me of Fred Astaire doing his famous broom routine in the movie *Royal Wedding*.

Even this far south the winter days were short. We met up back at camp that first evening, prepped dinner, and gathered firewood, and before the sun set Dowtin, who offers full three-day courses in the instinctive shooting method at a club in Phoenix, gave us a short clinic and a gunslingerlike demonstration using a hand skeet thrower we had brought along. Then we built a fire of mesquite and oak, and when the wood had burned down to red-hot coals we grilled venison tenderloin that Collector had brought from Colorado.

It had been a long drive and a long day, and we had three more to go. Straws were drawn to see who got the spare bed in the Airstream, who slept on the floor, and who in the tent.

Flights of geese and myriads of the blue quail (scaled quail) were seen, and flocks of turkeys from which we got one. The river bed at the junction of the San Pedro was seamed with tracks of

deer and turkey; some signs of beaver and one trail of wild hogs
(javelina.)
—Lt. William Hemsley Emory (1848)

Early accounts of the country by the first white trappers and explorers almost never fail to mention the profligacy of quail— huge coveys of a thousand Gambel's were not uncommon. But such numbers can only be supported by prime habitat, and by all accounts the Arizona uplands were far more luxuriant then— immense open grasslands that have largely been succeeded in the past centuries by noxious shrubs and woody scrub, mesquite, creosote, and saltbush.

Bovine grazing of the rich grasses has a long and checkered history; before being driven out once and for all by the fierce Apaches in the 1830s, the Spanish maintained a flourishing cattle industry in southern Arizona as early as the late 1600s. Then many of the rivers, streams, and springs that now run only seasonally ran year-round and were full of beaver and fat Gila trout (actually a species of chub). There were dense forests of tall-growth timber in the river bottoms, extensive wetlands, and rich black soil in the floodplains.

Of wildlife, the early explorers to the region reported turkeys, ducks, geese, elk, deer, bears, javelina, wolves, coyotes, bobcats, mountain lions, pronghorn antelope, bighorn sheep, et al. And, of course, as mentioned, literally millions of quail. The good news is that with the obvious exception of grizzlies and wolves, all of these species are still extant on the San Carlos Apache Reservation (bighorn sheep, extirpated from the region by the early 1900s, have recently been reintroduced), and record book big game is still taken there.

If centuries of overgrazing have exacted a devastating toll on the Arizona landscape and its wildlife, so have the activities of timbering, mining, and farming. Endless water impoundments, diversion, and pumping have transformed both the former riparian ecosystem as well as the lush native grasses of the dry-

lands. As a result Arizona is widely considered by ecologists to be the most radically altered natural state in the lower forty-eight. And man is not the only culprit; there is ample evidence that the climate in the region has been significantly drier in this past century.

Curiously, and perhaps symptomatic of a system that has failed them, very few Apaches live in the country any longer; they mostly live in town, and but for the ubiquitous cattle and a few old abandoned homes and ranches there is very little sign of human presence to mar the immense landscape. The desert still owns a stark, crystalline beauty, especially at dawn or during one of the Southwest's justly celebrated sunsets, when the vast open reaches and the distant surrounding mountains, the buttes and rock formations, seem particularly grand and impermeable dressed in their breathtaking rainbow hues. In the foothills and mountains rising from the desert floor, rivers and springs still flow through steep canyons and lush bottoms of cottonwoods, sycamores, willows, and oaks.

On our next day, after a particularly strenuous hunt, we swam in a hot spring along the San Carlos River. It was a verdant, idyllic spot that recalled something of the former splendor of the land—though sunken cans and beer bottles were sad reminders of the hard realities of rez life in our own times.

And there were still quail to be found, if not quite in the fecundity of pioneer days or even the coveys of former years as described by Dowtin and Hopkins. We worked for our birds; there would be no hanging around camp in the afternoons because we had limited out in the morning. It was tough, physical hunting, both in the scorched desert flats for scaled quail and in the cow-burnt drylands and rocky slopes above, where we chased the fleet-footed running Gambel's. It was especially hard on the dogs—the birds didn't hold for their points, and the malpai rock worked like pumice on their pads; the mesquite bloodied their noses, and prickly pear cactus spines protruded from their faces like porcupine quills; fallen pieces of cholla cac-

tus attached themselves to their feet, hobbling them so completely that they would stop dead in their tracks and wait for someone to come extricate them.

We feasted today (Oct. 24) on blue quail (scaled quail) and
teal, and at night Stanly came in with a goose.
—Lt. William Helmsley Emory (1848)

On the last morning we hunted scalies in the desert flats. Driving out, we passed a stock tank around which stood four starving horses heartbreakingly gaunt, swaybacked, swollen-bellied beasts—and as we were hunting we came upon a fifth, too weak to lift its drooping head. "If I had a handgun with me, I'd shoot that horse," Dowtin said disgustedly. "You'd be doing it a favor."

We had a successful morning hunt of mixed scalies and Gambel's, everyone bringing in birds. Hopkins and Dowtin had to get home to Flagstaff that evening, and we said our good-byes back at the truck. I knew that they were embarrassed about not producing more birds for us in their home territory, but no one cared, as we had all been in that situation before and it had been a fine trip nevertheless. We exchanged addresses, promising another hunt, another day.

The rest of our group spent a final night camped on the rez. As we were grilling our quail over the fire, we saw headlights from a vehicle turn off the highway onto the road that led down to our camp. The car came to a stop, engine idling. It remained there on the hillside above us for some time, long enough to make us uneasy. I am sorry to say this, but there is a distinct third world feel to many native American reservations, especially those that have not yet been falsely assimilated into our economic culture by legalized gambling. Sovereign lands, the Apache reservations of Arizona, like those of the northern Cheyenne and the Sioux to the north, are as different from our world as another country altogether. And, unless one is a hunter or a fisherman there is much cause to visit them. The few non-

native Americans who have occasion to cross these borders are usually tourists on their way someplace else and rarely get out of their cars. They hurry through, careful to have a full tank of gas, praying that they don't break down, relieved when they finally cross back into their own country.

Now Doug Baer said, "I think I'll get my shotgun. Just in case whoever that is comes into camp. You never know. From all these bottles they obviously have parties down here, and someone may have been drinking." Baer, a Vietman veteran, has spent a good deal of time in and around Indian reservations all over the West. Now a couple more of us slipped off quietly on similar missions—which may certainly be perceived in certain circles as melodramatic, possibly even paranoiac.

Finally the phantom car started slowly down the road toward our camp. When it pulled up, we saw with some relief that it was an official reservation vehicle. A uniformed Apache man stepped out of the driver's side and flipped on a spotlight, which he shoned into each of our faces in turn, so that we had to put our arms up or turn away from the glare.

"Where's your fifth man?" he inquired.

Dave Christian, who along with Williams had not armed himself, stepped from the shadows. "I'm right here," he said. "I was taking a piss."

"Who are you?" one of us asked the Apache.

"Mike Randall," he said. "I'm the game warden. I need to check your hunting permits."

Someone laughed with relief. "You can turn that light off, Mike," someone else said. "We're just here to hunt your quail. And we're legal."

We produced our licenses and invited Randall to join us around the fire. "I watched you from up there through my starlight night glasses," he said. "I never come into somebody's camp until I know how many people are there and what they are doing," he explained. Then he chuckled. "I watched you all go get your guns." But Randall didn't seem to hold it against us,

either. Who knows better than the American Indian not to be taken by surprise in one's own camp?

We offered the game warden a beer, but he asked for a cup of coffee instead. "I quit drinking a few years ago," he said. "I'm not a sociable drinker. In those days I would come down here and drink all your beer and when you ran out I would make you go get more and if you didn't . . ." He paused, smiled, and added very softly, "I would get mad."

Randall told us that he'd formerly been a reservation police-man and that he found the game warden business pretty tame. "I like action," he said. "I like family fights." I wondered if the warden was disappointed that the white men bird hunters had been so cooperative.

"You find any quail?" he asked.

"A few, not too many."

"Too bad you didn't ask me first," he said. "I know where there are plenty of quail."

"We have extra birds for dinner," I offered. "Why don't you stay and eat with us?"

Randall made a face of distaste. "Quail is white man food," he said disdainfully. "I like elk."

The game warden drank his coffee and said that he'd better be getting home. "Next time you come here, you call me," he said, handing me a piece of paper. "Here's my address and phone number. You can park next to my mobile home. You can hook your trailer up there. I'll show you where all the quail you want are."

We watched as Randall drove slowly back out the rutted two-track, the beams from his headlights bouncing wildly off the trees.

"It's just a lucky thing that you guys got your guns ready," said Williams in a mildly mocking tone. "Just in case we had to have a shootout with Night-eyes Randall, the renegade Apache game warden."

"You never know," Baer said. "Remember what he said: in

the old days he would come down here and drink all our beer and if we didn't go get more for him, he would get mad. Then you'd have wished you were armed, trust me."

"I'd have just gone and gotten him some more beer," Williams replied.

"Yeah? Well, do you know how the Apaches used to like to torture their enemies?" I added. "I've been reading up. They'd stake them to anthills out in the desert and rub wild honey over their genitals, mouth, and eyes, and then they'd sit around watching and laughing as the red ants dined. Or if there were trees around they'd tie a man by the ankles and hoist him up from a limb until his head was just a few inches from the ground. Then they'd build a fire under his head, keeping it just the right temperature, so that it wouldn't kill the man right away but would very slowly cook his brain until his skull exploded."

"Aren't those quail ready yet?" someone asked.

White man food or not, our dinner of freshly killed quail, marinated and grilled over mesquite coals, was superb—redolent of the wildness of the desert. We were heading out the next morning, back across the border to our own country. It gets cold in Apache land at night in the wintertime, and we closed in tighter around the glowing embers of the fire.

SPRING

18

DINNER

That's right you're not from Texas,
That's right you're not from Texas,
That's right you're not from Texas,
But Texas wants you anyway.
                              —Lyle Lovett

I drove it in two very long days, Arizona to Florida, 1,800 miles. God, you think you're never going to get out of Texas; you're in the state so long that you nearly establish residency. But I was determined to get to Florida in time for dinner the second evening.

Dinner that first night at my friend Guy's farm near Tallahassee consisted of three scaled and three Gambel's quail from the desert and three bobwhite quail from the farm. As another bird-hunting friend, Jim Harrison, likes to remark at such unique culinary events, "Who else in America is eating this meal for dinner tonight?"

I had brought the southwestern quail with me "in the feath-

ers," as were Guy's bobwhite, and before we plucked the birds we laid them all along the kitchen counter to admire them, to examine and compare feathering, crop contents, general size, age, sex, and weight—all the small, layman's observations that bring added dimension to the hunt. I had also brought some chunks of mesquite wood with me from the desert, and these we laid atop the native oak that was already burning in the fireplace until all was melded together into hot coals. Then we watched the quail turning on the spit, dripping and browning. On the table each species tasted as distinct as the country in which they lived, the Arizona quail with a slightly more pungent, wilder flavor than the bobwhite.

How strange it seemed, like a dream, to wake up my first morning in Florida to a dense fog settled over the massive live oaks that were hung in Spanish moss like oxidized tinsel, to be hunting through a classic southern pine forest as the sun finally parted the mist. In that peculiar state of road lag, the dry spareness of the desert I had just left still lived on in my mind's eye, like the fading afterimage on a television screen, not quite replaced yet by this new, lush country.

But I was only passing through and it was even stranger, a bit over a week later, to find myself at dawn in a snipe marsh on the southern end of Lake Okeechobee. It was late in the season, and it occurred to me that I had begun and ended my hunting year—which, of course, does not follow the calendar year—shooting snipe, way back on the first day of September near my home in Colorado, where Sweetz and I spend our time slogging through the marshes formed by beaver dams along a river bottom in a high mountain park. The country there could not conceivably be more different from the flat watery Everglades—an exotic, tropical land of palmettos and alligators and water lilies, of mysterious Indian shell mounds hidden in dense, vine-covered oak forests, of feral hogs and wild lemon trees.

One day I came upon one of these lemon trees and I picked some fruit from it, and later at the local clapboard country store

I asked the old "cracker" proprietor if he knew who might have planted these lemon trees in the woods and when. He shrugged, as if not much interested in the question, and answered, "Stool trees," and when he saw my confused expression he added, "Couple hundred years ago the Seminole Indians lived in these swamps: they'd eat a lemon and then they'd shit out the seeds in the woods. Those trees grew up out of their stools. That's why we call 'em stool trees."

I was supposed to hunt ducks that morning, but in riding around in a swamp buggy the afternoon before I had watched a dozen alligators sunning themselves on the banks of the river, not far away from the ponds where the duck blinds were set. Not far enough away for me and Sweetz, in any case. Big gators, some of them—gnarled, vicious-looking, prehistoric creatures ten to twelve feet long—plenty big enough to look upon a yellow Lab swimming for a duck retrieve as a delicious plump appetizer, a pig in a blanket, say. I've heard scores of horror stories on the subject, how the gator comes up from beneath and yanks the dog under the surface, the way a bass hits a top-water plug, drags the flailing, drowning dog down to a dark underwater lair where the creature stashes the corpse until the flesh has aged and rotted to its taste. No thank you. Surely no duck on earth is worth that terrifying prospect. So Sweetz and I begged off the duck hunt and were dropped before dawn in the snipe marsh instead. It was beautiful there with the shorebirds and marsh dwellers winging heavily overhead when it was still barely light enough to see them, the marsh waking up with all its jungle noises.

In this way the snipe formed bookends to Sweetzer's and my hunting season, the first and the last bird shot and retrieved, one in Colorado, the other in Florida. It seemed nearly impossible to me and at the same time wondrous that the same species could inhabit such radically different ecosystems, the same bird with the same crazy zigzagging pattern of flight and the same high haunting tones as the air rushes through their wing feath-

ers—a sound as lonesome as can be—as they rise skyward from the boggy earth and tumble, or don't tumble, to our gun.

That night for dinner at the ranch house beside which we were camped we ate wild pig lathered with a paste made of fresh herbs, garlic, and olive oil and slow-roasted in the oven. We ate freshly killed snipe, grilled pink, and medallions of wild venison tenderloin sautéed quickly with onions, and deep-fried alligator tail onto which we squeezed the tart juice of wild lemons, planted, as we now know, by Seminole Indians.

Which begs the question: who else in America is eating this meal for dinner tonight?

19

MY LIFE AS A BUMP ON A LOG

In spite of all I have read about the wild turkey being the "ultimate game bird," I've never had much interest in hunting them. My passion for upland game birds has always been quite specific to those species that can be hunted with a dog. At the same time, turkey hunting has always seemed a bit too sedentary to suit me. Finally, I have deeply mixed feelings about spring hunting of any kind. To my way of thinking spring is the season of rebirth, of courtship and mating and rearing of young. This is surely a mushy, sentimental notion, but the act of hunting seems somehow contradictory to the spirit of spring. And I think a fella ought to be able to go out in the springtime when the hormones are kicking in and strut his stuff for the ladies without having to worry about getting his damn head blown off.

However, on a purely practical level, it's quite true that spring is the season when the infamously wily wild turkey can be called in to the gun and if the hunter is man enough to go out in the woods and coax a puffed-up gobbler into range by making the

alluring sounds of a horny hen, I say more power to him—get in touch with your feminine side, boys. . . .

So for all my niggling reservations about the sport, when my attorney friend Ken Beall invited me out to south central Florida to hunt Osceola turkeys I wasn't about to say no. Beall is an experienced turkey hunter and an incredibly energetic man, who moves through life on fast-forward. I figured if he can sit still long enough to hunt turkeys so could I.

Two weeks before our scheduled hunt he had me over to his house to watch turkey-hunting videos and gave me a list of gear I would require. Then he demonstrated his calling techniques, which I must admit had I been an eligible bachelor gobbler would have melted my heart. "Have you ever been so successful at calling a turkey in that he's actually tried to mount you?" I asked Ken.

Beall considered the question with perfect lawyerly detachment. "That's never happened to me personally," he answered deadpan, "but I have heard of others with that level of skill."

Now Beall was rapping smartly on my door at five o'clock on the morning of our hunt. I slipped into my brand-new camo outfit and thus virtually invisible slipped stealthily out of the cabin, Sweetz distraught, incredulous that she wasn't to be allowed to come: *What's wrong with this picture? He's wearing camo, he's carrying a shotgun, and he's leaving me behind?* It was a moment without precedent in her life as a Labrador retriever.

By the first faint light of day I was sitting with my back against a tree deep in the forest on the edge of a small clearing in the middle of the most beautiful oak hammock imaginable. I was beginning to like turkey hunting. The live oaks were huge overhead, their twisted, knotty branches sprouting lush green ferns and mosses of all varieties. The sky was lightening slowly to the east, the forest coming alive with spring sounds. Hundreds of birds took up their morning songs. I watched a tiny tree frog no larger than my thumbnail as it hunkered down on the branch of a thorny vine inches from my face. The frog, too, was hunt-

ing, so perfectly camouflaged that it looked exactly like a small bump on the vine. I felt a true kinship with it and hoped that I was as well concealed.

With daylight I tried out my Knight and Hale "Fighting Purr" system—two push-button calls that the hunter operates one in each hand, thereby imitating the sounds of a pair of turkeys squabbling over territory. Because all that raging testosterone has the gobblers on the fight as well as on the prowl to get laid, these calls are supposed to make the birds come running in to mix it up with their rivals. I hadn't had time to learn the diaphragm mouth call wherein lies the true art of turkey hunting, and being a bit uncomfortable with the idea of deceiving a hotblooded gobbler by promising romance only to kill him instead, I preferred to pass myself off as a competitor rather than as a sex object. Now I felt curiously like a puppeteer as my left hand argued with my right—they were a couple of pissed-off roosters ready to rumble. I immediately got the attention of a busybody crow who flew over to see what the ruckus was about; it hopped around on the branches above me, cawing crankily. Soon a squirrel living in my oak tree came out to complain about all the noise, hissing and spitting and growling. Other squirrels in the forest took up the alarm like a gang of querulous monkeys.

As humans we tend to view wildlife primarily as it flees from our clumsy approach, and I realized what a rare perspective the turkey hunter enjoys, observing the natural world as a proverbial fly on the wall. Except for periodically operating my calls with my index fingers, I sat virtually motionless beneath that oak tree for nearly five hours. I'm not going to tell you that I didn't have moments of antsiness, but the longer I sat there, the more attuned I seemed to become, the more engaged and absorbed. Time seemed to pass as if in some alternate dimension.

At one point a large wild boar shuffled out of the underbrush into the clearing thirty feet or so away from me, close enough that I could smell him—a dank, musty, pungent scent. He was brindle-colored and had brutish curved tusks, and he made an

ominous low grunting noise like a grumpy old man talking to himself. I don't believe he saw me, but I'm sure he, in turn, smelled me, and I had a fast adrenaline rush remembering Ken Beall's wild hog stories of the evening before: a friend charged and gored, his femoral artery severed, nearly bled to death, another also gored, coming within millimeters of a permanent gig with the eunuch choir. Trying not to reveal myself, I looked around for the nearest climbable tree. Grumbling and grunting and snorting, the boar continued on his way.

A bit later (or it may have been hours), I was working my calls when a Cooper's hawk flew into the top of my oak tree to investigate. Possibly he hoped to be the beneficiary in case of injuries in the ongoing turkey fight. When I stopped calling, he got curious, flapping down to a lower branch only a few feet away from me. He cocked his head back and forth, looking around on the ground, clearly perplexed: where the hell did those turkeys go? I remained motionless; like the frog, I aspired to be a bump on the tree. The hawk looked right at me; he looked right in my eyes. In spite of his famous hawk vision, he did not see me. I was a bump on the tree.

20

THE OLD MAN AND HIS SEA

The old saw has it that we go through life with a diminishing portfolio of interests until eventually we reach the stage when our recreational activities have winnowed down to looking after our own decrepit bodies. And then we die. In the hopes of staving off this discouraging scenario (although I don't suppose there's much we can do about the dying part), I believe that it's prudent to make regular deposits in one's portfolio of interests—kind of like yearly 401K deposits. It was in this spirit that I took up, this past spring, two new sports—turkey hunting and surf fishing.

Actually, a friend had recently made me the gift of a brand-new surf-casting outfit, and so I felt obligated to take it up, even though the last thing in the world I really need is more stuff to cart around—especially big stuff like a surf rod, which even broken down in its case takes up nearly as much room in the Airstream as another passenger. Then, of course, there's all the other stuff you need to go with it.

I went right down to the local tackle store and got the es-

sentials—some leader and hook rigs, swivels, sinkers, and bait—and I asked some advice of the old fellow who had owned and operated the tackle shop for the past fifty-six years. It was a wonderful place with ancient lures and other dusty items on the wall that I recognized from my childhood. Unfortunately, running the shop had kept the proprietor kind of busy over the years; he admitted that he hadn't been surf-fishing himself since 1957 and that most of his old surf-fishing customers were retired from the sport—indeed, many of them were casting in the big surf in the sky. Still, the old fellow knew plenty of interesting angling lore. The truth is that the sport hasn't changed that much, other than the depressingly familiar fact that on the east coast of Florida, at least, due to a variety of causes that include pollution, ubiquitous beachfront development, and commercial overfishing, the surf fishing isn't nearly as good as it once was. The good news is that there are a number of marine and sport-fishing organizations, fighting (successfully in some cases) this insidious downward spiral.

There are still fish to be caught out there, and soon I was prowling the beaches, sometimes getting up before dawn and walking down to the end of the block to fish my "home" water for a couple of hours before the day's work, sometimes driving an hour or farther to reach more pristine beaches, where I also made the acquaintance of other, more experienced surf casters. Though they tend to be a somewhat solitary lot, each with a carefully staked out and inviolable territory, some of them, I learned, were simply lonely retirees who, though they might posture a bit at first, were delighted to have an interested protégé to whom they could hold forth on the finer points of their sport.

And soon I was catching fish. Maybe the best thing about surf fishing is that you never really know what you're going to haul from the sea—depending on the season and the area—permit, pompano, mackerel, jacks, barracuda, snook, tarpon, grunts, snappers, bluefish. Sure, maybe I haven't caught all of those species from the beach yet, but I've caught a few and I'm

working on the others. I've released a bunch of fish, and I've enjoyed a few fish dinners, too. My sensory experience has run the gamut from the infuriatingly delicate taps of little blue runners effectively stripping my bait to having my rod nearly ripped out of my arms by muscular jacks that hit like charging bulls. And I have a new surf-fishing mentor, too—a wise old fellow named Ben, a retiree from the garment business in New York, who is teaching me everything he knows about the sport.

Ben's been at it for a while, and he has all the right stuff. The first day I showed up on his beach, I had only my new rod-and-reel outfit and a red plastic beach pail with my bait in it. I had found the pail in the garage, and I must say carrying it down the beach I felt just like a twelve-year-old kid, especially when I saw Ben there with all of his great stuff. He had one of those white five-gallon plastic paint buckets, which are absolutely *de rigueur* for the serious surf fisherman. Hanging on the outside of the bucket were his sundry leader, hook, and sinker arrangements—exotic custom things that he rigged himself (and about which he would be rather stingy teaching me). He had one of those low-to-the-ground webbed beach chairs with his rod in a PVC rod holder stuck in the sand beside it. He had a beach umbrella and a cooler with his bait on ice and with cold drinks and sandwiches in it. He had a beautiful slab of driftwood that he used as a cutting board, shiny with fish scales and a fine old much-sharpened, weathered-handled fillet knife on it. He had a canvas bag full of magazines and paperbacks (he favored Travis McGee mysteries, which immediately gave us something in common, as I am an old fan of the late John D. McDonald) and the day's *New York Times*. Well, you can just about imagine how Ben smirked that first day at the new kid with his little red beach pail. . . .

Slowly, not all at once, so as to avoid appearing to be too much of a dude, I started getting some of my own stuff. First I ditched the red pail and got a five-gallon bucket; pretty soon I had my own chair, though I still preferred to walk up and down

the beach and fish from a standing position, which Ben considered an enormous waste of energy but which was certainly more entertaining for Sweetz, who usually accompanied me on these excursions.

To me the best times to surf-fish are the first couple hours after dawn and the last hour or so before dark—the beaches are usually deserted then, and the Florida light is spectacular. I'm not sure it makes for the best fishing, but I love it when a west wind is blowing, flattening the ocean to an absolute dead calm. Sometimes then at dusk or at dawn I'll watch huge schools of bait fish boiling just offshore, a line of them as far as I can see up and down the beach, birds wheeling in the air working them from above and larger fish busting them from below, all of us part of the food chain.

Unlike Ben, who, after all, is retired and a widower and has nothing much else to do, I rarely stay out all day. He claims that midday has its special charms, not the least of them being the bikini-clad women on the beach, who to Ben's mind more than compensate for the lull in the fishing. "I may be old, kid," he says, "but I'm not dead." One day when I stayed later than usual and we were reading Travis McGee mysteries side by side, Ben suddenly said, "Get ready, kid!" I thought maybe the crafty old angler had spotted a fish about to hit one or another of our baits, but actually he was alerting me to the approach of a young lady jogging up the beach wearing a skimpy thong suit. "Now you tell me," he said with satisfaction as she came even. "Which would you rather look at in the middle of March, a broad walking down Fifth Avenue all bundled up in a fur coat or that?"

Ben is at the beach nearly every day, weather permitting— and even sometimes not permitting. He walks over from his condo, which is only a few blocks from the ocean, carrying his beach chair, canvas beach bag, and rod and bait bucket and with an enormous stogie in his mouth. Ben always plants his stuff on exactly the same vertical line on the beach, a line that moves forward or back depending on the tide. Ben's spot, this movable

line is called by the other local anglers—all primarily cranky, nut-brown, bandy-legged old men, with the odd cranky, nut-brown, bandy-legged old woman thrown in. One time before I'd gotten to know him I inadvertently tried to pitch my fishing camp on "Ben's spot" before he'd arrived at the beach for the day. You'd have thought I'd tried to take up squatter's rights in the old man's condo by the chewing out I got from his peers— they descended on me from all sides like a flock of squawking gulls.

Ben's beach is a bit of a drive for me, and all winter I'd been trying to talk him into fishing some other beaches with me, up or down the coast, but Ben is very stubborn about his home water. "Kid," he always asks when I bring up the subject, "does the ocean look the same from those other beaches?" I allow as how, yeah, it looks more or less the same. "Is the fishing better there than it is here?" he asks.

"Sometimes it's better; sometimes it's not," I answer. "Depends on how the fish are running."

"Same variety of fish?"

"Yup. Pretty much."

"Kid, I've been fishing this beach for over ten years. Nearly every day of my retired life. I like it here. My friends are here. Now you tell me, why do I want to get in the car and drive all the way to hell and back when I can just walk right down here to my spot and catch fish?"

Well, sure, I could see Ben's point, but still I always tried to explain to him that maybe he should try another spot just for the simple change of pace it offers—just to see some new water, even if it does look more or less the same. And who knows? Depending on how the fish are running on any given day maybe the fishing might be better elsewhere. Once I even tried to tempt Ben with the lure of a fishing trip to a nearby nude beach, but he was scarily pragmatic about that, too. "Kid," he said, "I think that there are plenty of good reasons to get naked, even for an old fart like me who without his clothes on looks like a

shriveled orange peel left out in the sun. But trust me on this one," he added, nodding sagely. "Fishing and nude don't mix."

One thing you finally come to understand when you hang around with older people for any length of time is that they hate change; many of them want things to stay pretty much the way they are. And that's just how it was on the day when I broke out my fly rod in front of Ben for the first time. Truthfully, I'd grown a bit tired of conventional surf casting, especially the way Ben practices it—from the comfort of his beach chair. When he saw me rigging my fly rod, you'd have thought I'd hauled out a bag of dynamite sticks to lob into the sea. "What in the *hell* are you going to do with that *goddamn* thing?" he wanted to know, poking his cigar crankily at my rod.

"I want to try out a new fly that my friend Jimbo is trying," I answered. "He tells me the pompano up his way go nuts for it." I handed Ben one of the flies.

"Why, that looks just like a sand flea," he said.

"Yeah, that's what it's supposed to look like."

"So why don't you just go down to edge of the water and catch some real sand fleas, big shot?" Ben said, his old person's Pavlovian response toward change kicking in.

"Well, because they'd come right off the hook when you tried to cast them with a fly rod," I explained.

"And that's exactly why on this beach, Mr. River-Runs-Through-It, we use surf-casting rods," Ben said smugly.

"Yeah? Well, you're forgetting one other thing, Ben."

"What's that, kid?"

"You're forgetting how hard it's gotten to find live sand fleas around here anymore."

This was quite true and Ben knew it. Up until a few years ago it was nothing to walk along the edge of the sea and collect a bucketful of sand fleas in no time. But recently they seemed, like far too many other things on this finite earth of ours, to be getting scarcer and scarcer, until most anglers hereabouts, Ben included, had virtually given up using them for bait.

Now I rigged up two of Jimbo's sand flea flies, using one as a dropper. I was casting a sink tip line with a short leader, and I worked a good loop out over the choppy sea while Ben watched me skeptically from his beach chair. One thing about fly casting from the beach is that you really have to watch your backcast, lest you accidentally hook yourself a mermaid, as Ben sometimes calls the young women on the beach. Finally I dropped the line on the surface, made a slow ten-count while the flies sank, and then retrieved them slowly, bumping the sand fleas along the bottom. *Wham!* a pompano hit almost immediately, *wham!*— another one—now I had two on at once. Pompano are not big fish, but relative to their length they have a large body surface and create a lot of water resistance—with a light fly rod it was kind of like fighting two swimming skillets. I looked back at Ben, his rod straight in its holder; he was scowling a little, his arms crossed on his chest, cigar clamped between his teeth. He was clearly annoyed that the kid was catching fish in his sea using an unauthorized, unapproved method.

But just then, as if he had suddenly remembered his own younger days, before things had narrowed down quite so much, Ben smiled at me through his scowl, seemed in an instant to shed a decade or more of age. He took his cigar out of his mouth, waved it heartily in the air, and called out: "Hey, kid, way to go! *Way to go!*"

21

GUIDE SCHOOL

He moves across the ocean flats as easily as another man walks on land, lifting each foot clear of the water and putting it down again, toe pointed, knifing through the surface, barely creating a wake—perfect grace that looks like dance as much as sport. "The quieter you can get there," he explains, "the better." He speaks softly, in a lilting voice with just the faintest trace of an English accent, a remnant from the dark colonial days. "You make noise, and they're gone."

Allan "J. J." Dames Jr. is stalking bonefish on the flats of Grand Exuma, Bahamas. "See those little green holes in the sand?" Dames says, pointing. "Those are fresh bonefish tracks— less than five minutes old. That's where they dig for crabs. The blue holes are old tracks, and the big holes are manta ray tracks." Too, this is hunting as much as fishing; one need only squint one's eyes a bit and let the imagination run to see in Dames's precise, elegant motions the hunter stalking game on the Serengeti with a spear or on the Great Plains with bow and arrow— the purely organic fit of man to environment.

But, of course, we're hard on the twenty-first century, and in this case J. J. Dames, former auto mechanic and a third-generation flats guide, is hunting bonefish with a high-tech Loomis graphite fly rod—a convenient and apparently mutually agreeable marriage of cultures.

For those of us white boys who have been flailing the American waters for trout most of our lives and are currently sloshing noisily behind him through the Bahamian flats in our Orvis wading booties, watching Dames fish can be a deeply humbling experience. He has been fly-casting himself for a mere year and a half, yet he throws a line as effortlessly as a pro. "I'm the worst caster of the guides," he tells us modestly.

"Yeah, right, J. J."

He laughs a deep, warm, infectious, "*He, he, he, he.*" "No, really," he says. "You should see some of the others."

In fact, the guides at Peace & Plenty Bonefish Lodge on Grand Exuma Island have learned from the best—world champion fly caster Steve Rajeff, who puts on several clinics here a season. There is not one of the native students, according to lodge owner Bob Hyde, who can't throw a hundred feet of fly line, nor has there ever been a student in the short history of Hyde's three-year-old guide school who hasn't immediately taken to the sport. "They have natural timing," Hyde explained, which to the politically correct may seem like a racist remark, equivalent to saying that the Bahamians have "natural rhythm." Which, I'm afraid, they do. "And they have no inhibitions," added Hyde. Not to mention that they simply love to do it; after a full day of guiding sports on the water, the guides often get together on the beach at the end of the day just to practice casting together—probably a welcome release from watching their rich American charges whip the flats all day long.

Now Dames spots bonefish moving, way out beyond the range of the visitor's vision. With two tidy false casts he has seventy feet of line in the air, releases it, crouches low, strips, strips,

strips, and then with a final definitive strip sets the hook, raises the rod tip: the bonefish runs, the reel shrieks . . .

When Bob Hyde, a flats fishing guide in the Florida Keys, first moved over to Grand Exuma Island in the Bahamas nearly four years ago it was with the idea in mind of retiring. He'd been seventeen years in the keys, during which time he had watched the sport of flats fishing boom in popularity, the number of guides and the pressure on the flats expanding exponentially. What had been in the early days of the sport a good-natured competition among guides to reach the best flats first had gradually deteriorated into an inherently violent territorialism. "It got to the point that fistfights were breaking out at the dock," Hyde remembers with an astonished laugh. Hyde had been fishing in the Exumas during the summer for years, and now with his kids grown and out of the house it occurred to him that he didn't need to put up with the keys scene any longer.

But Hyde—a fit, energetic, articulate forty-nine-year-old man with piercing blue eyes and a keen intelligence—is clearly not a good candidate for lounging around on the beach sipping coconut juice. He and his wife Karen's life in Grand Exuma has been anything but retirement for the past four years.

Now J. J. Dames is spotting and pointing bonefish for us. We're wading Rolle Town Flat. It is a heartbreakingly beautiful spot. Defined by arcing shoreline on one side, the vast expanse of sea runs the full blue-green color spectrum all the way to the skyline, punctuated in the middle distance by corral islands that to a westerner have something the look of small herds of bison humped up on the plains. The water on the flats itself is only about calf-deep on a falling tide; and though I have been forbidden by editorial directive to ever again use the cliché *gin-clear water*, perhaps I may be allowed to say that the sea on

these flats is as clear as cold vodka and ruffled by the wind. Manta rays ghost by on the sandy bottom like aquatic spaceships, and herds of bonefish patrol the flats in perfect formation like small silver submarines.

I wanted to watch Dames do it first, in order to see it done properly, perfectly, and now it is my turn. Possibly because I fish so rarely with guides, I tend to think of them less as employees— facilitators in my immediate efforts to catch fish—and more as interpreters of strange lands, educators who, if I pay close-enough attention, might impart to me some small measure of their hard-earned knowledge.

J. J. Dames, like all of the guides at Peace & Plenty Bonefish Lodge, grew up on the water; he's been handlining bonefish for fun since he was eight years old, so when he tells you something about the habits of the fish, you listen.

He stops and bends over the water and slowly lowers his hand to grasp something in the sand. He brings it up, opening his palm to reveal a small cigar (pronounced "sigger") crab, the main food source for bonefish. "The crabs come up in the flats for the sun," he explains, "and the bonefish follow them."

An informal flats guiding service had existed since the early sixties on Grand Exuma, and Bob Hyde had fished here over the years with all of the old-timers, as well as their younger successors. Using these guides as a nucleus, he started his own operation slowly, running two or three boats a day out of the Peace & Plenty Beach Hotel, which was managed by his old friend and partner, American hotelier Charlie Pflueger.

Today, only a few short years later, Hyde has better than a dozen guides working for him, Peace & Plenty Bonefish Lodge is Exuma's largest employer, and guiding is above and away the best-paying job for men on the island. It seems that Hyde and the burgeoning sportfishing industry came along at a propitious time; the new Bahamian government had recently and effec-

tively shut down the island's former largest and best-paying industry—the illicit drug-running trade.

"There they are," Dames says. "See them, about a hundred feet out, heading this way?"

We're crouched, shoulder to shoulder, but I don't see the fish right away. Then I do, cruising in formation right at us. Blow the cast and they scatter like a busted covey of quail. Now the adrenaline starts pumping. "Start your cast" Dames instructs. He senses my nerves, my body vibrating like a tuning fork. "Relax. No problem," he whispers. "OK, now, pop it!"

Early on, with financial aid in the form of scholarships from the Benjamin Foundation (named after another of Hyde's partners) Bob Hyde began sending some of the young men from Exuma to the Florida Keys Fly Fishing School, run by his friend Sandy Moret in Islamorado. At the same time, Hyde started a guide school of his own on the island—a twelve-week program covering everything from knot tying, to small-engine repair, to casting, to social skills. Like J. J. Dames, most of Hyde's Bahamian students already knew plenty about bonefish, but they didn't know much about the sport of fly fishing and even less about the cultural motivation of Americans willing to pay six or seven thousand dollars to come here to catch bonefish on a fly rod.

Hyde's guide school has since become a part of the local high school curriculum and has mushroomed into a full-blown vocational school in partnership with the Bahamian Ministry of Education and the College of the Bahamas. The school, with funding provided largely by the Benjamin Foundation, has recently moved into a new 3,000-square-foot building in George Town and now offers courses in electrical contracting, plumbing, and computer operation, with even more courses currently in development. Under the school's auspices a local island news-

paper, written and edited by the students, has been launched and funding provided for a mobile library. Not a bad piece of work for a man who claimed to be plotting his own retirement four years ago.

Back at the lodge at the end of the day, J. J. Dames teases me good-naturedly about my fishing skills, or lack thereof. The Bahamians possess a sweet, literal sense of humor that is entirely without cynicism, and now J. J. relates the story of my bad case of nerves on the flats, jostling me with an elbow in the ribs. "Man, you were so nervous your whole body was shaking, *he, he, he, he, he.*" He mimics my trembling, twitching all over like Elvis singing "Hound Dog." "*He, he, he, he, he, he.* . . . You wonder why I love this job?"

For all his accomplishments in the Exumas, Bob Hyde is quick to object to any portrayal of himself as some kind of island Robin Hood come to show the poor natives how to do things. He is, finally, a savvy businessman and entrepreneur, who understands the political and social wisdom of greasing the bureaucratic wheels, of giving back more than he takes.

"The most commonly asked questions that Americans ask me when they first get off the plane here," Hyde says "is 'how much is real estate and what kind of business can I open?' They have no understanding of the culture and no interest in learning anything about it."

Hyde's own deep respect and fondness for the Bahamians is clear in his easy interaction with the guides, whom he treats far more like friends and partners than employees. His operation represents ecotourism at its best—a fully symbiotic relationship, good for all parties, and benevolent to the environment. "They've been far more my savior than I have been theirs," Hyde says of his Bahamian hosts, with no trace of patronage.

"This has been the most enjoyable five years of my life. There's nothing philanthropic about it. We're making a little money, we're supporting the guides, and whatever's left over goes into the foundation. And we get to live someplace that we love. I laugh when I go back to the States now and see the culture there. I keep thinking: we've become the Jetsons!"

———

Yet another gorgeous day in the tropics, clear, with a stiff breeze on the water. Before we head out to the flats to fish with the youngest member of the Peace & Plenty staff, eighteen-year-old Garth Rolle, Steve Collector and I are visiting the oldest, seventy-four-year-old Will Rolle, in the tiny settlement of Rolle Town.

Set on a hillside overlooking the bay on one side, the open sea on the other, Rolle Town is an idyllic spot with brightly painted Bahamian cottages amid lush tropical foliage. It is well off the beaten tourist path, a town that visiting anglers rarely get to see, other than from the distant vantage point of Rolle Town Flat. It is here where many of the guides live or grew up.

Will Rolle was one of the island's original bonefish guides, taking up the profession in the early sixties; he used to fish with the legendary American angler Joe Brooks during his visits to Exuma. Rolle has known and fished with Bob Hyde for many years and still guides for Peace & Plenty two or three days a week. "Will chased me out of his boat years ago because I had a fly rod," Hyde had told me earlier with a laugh.

Today Will Rolle is himself an accomplished fly rodder and the patriarch of a kind of island bonefishing dynasty: not only is Garth (one of thirty grandchildren) a recent graduate of Hyde's guide school, but Will's son Michael, twenty-four, is also a member of the Peace & Plenty guide staff.

"I like to see the young people coming up," Will Rolle says as we stroll through Rolle Town, "because I'm going down. Guiding is a good job for them. It keeps them safe from doing

bad things. When the drug business was going on here it used to be that the young people wouldn't even look at you." Rolle pauses and looks out over the sea, smiling a gentle gap-toothed grin. "But we old fellows kept it up for them."

I ask Rolle a lame question: did he had ever attend the guide school himself or any of Steve Rajeff's casting clinics? "Oh, no, I never have," he answers softly, without irony. "They always have it on Wednesdays. I'm the church choirmaster, and that's the night we have practice. I'm not going to leave that to go to any kind of meeting." Will Rolle smiles and looks out again at the flats. "I know my way around pretty good out there," he says.

"Are you kidding?" said Hyde later with a hearty laugh. "Will *is* the guide school."

Garth Rolle is a quiet, polite young man, less gregarious than J. J. Dames, though no less keen about his fishing. Today, our last, we are fishing the flats in White Bay.

Hyde has set up an intricate rotational system, both to rest the flats against overfishing and to create a system of parity among the guides. As part of their training, each guide spends a solid two-week period sitting on and observing, in all tides and at all times of day, each of the sixty miles of flats that ring Grand Exuma. Each is then assigned a specific flat to fish, which eliminates competition among them to get to the best spot first—a lesson Hyde learned well during his years in the Florida Keys, when the morning run out to the flats sometimes resembled a professional bass tournament jump start. And there are, needless to say, no fistfights among the guides back at the dock at the end of the day.

Of late, young Garth Rolle had been scouting outlying flats with a pilot in a seaplane, as part of an experimental "flyout" program for the lodge. As we run out to the White Bay in the Boston whaler, he tells us something of the extraordinary things

he has seen—huge marlin in five feet of water, unnamed flats with ten-thousand tailing bonefish that have never seen an angler . . . pioneer tales.

We got a bit of a late start, the tide is running out fast and by the time we reach White Bay the water is literally only ankle-deep. Hundreds, maybe thousands of bonefish, are moving across the flat in schools of varying sizes, their tails exposed like sticks poking from the water. We watch Garth, fly rod in hand, stalk them. Crouching low with a suppleness known only to an eighteen-year-old, he drops to his knees and curls his torso to the water so that he seems to disappear, to become the water itself. Fish swim, unspooked and feeding, five feet away from him. "If you get your head down right to the water, it's easier to see their tails," he has explained. Something else learned—how to see, how to move, how to become. Now we watch as from this impossible contortionist posture the kid somehow manages a short perfect cast, a strip, a take, a hook up. The rest of the school zing away from him in all directions, as if he is the hub and their wakes, scribing the shallow water, are spokes on the wheel.

22

TORE DOWN BY SPORT

I don't know who first gave him the nickname Fishboy, but that's what everyone called him. I never did learn his real name. He wasn't even a boy—he was a full-grown man in his late twenties by the time I met him—but clearly he got the nickname when he was a kid for the simple reason that, because he fished so much, he'd practically become a fish himself. In fact, he had vaguely fishlike features—wide-set goggly eyes and slightly pursed lips. I have a totally unproven theory that sometimes people spend so much time thinking about and pursuing a certain sport that they begin to resemble their chosen game—the bear hunter begins to look, and act, like a bear, the mountain lion hunter like a cat, the trout fisherman like a trout. The transformation happens, goes my theory, from trying so hard to think like another species that one actually in a sense becomes it. I wouldn't be a bit surprised if one day Fishboy just slipped into the water and joined the bass.

That was his specialty, bass fishing, but Fishboy was one of the most consummate all-around sportsmen that I've ever

known—and I've known a bunch of them. He could do it all; he owned the pure genetic ability to figure out how things worked in the outdoors. It's an enviable talent, a form of genius, like being a musical prodigy. But being able to think like wild things doesn't always come without a price.

I met Fishboy one morning in a tackle store in a small town in southern Georgia. It was mid-April and the new leaves were sprouting on the live oak trees, an intensely bright shade of green, the dogwoods in full bloom, the earth coming back to life with the lush fecundity that only a southern spring knows. I was only passing through, looking, as usual, for a little sport— in this case, information on bass fishing in the area.

I was inquiring about the local fishing opportunities of the proprietor of the tackle shop when Fishboy sidled up alongside me. "I could probably take you out fishing," he whispered, "in the river . . . for bream and bass. You understand what *a'm* sayin'?"

"You a guide?" I asked.

"He doesn't have a guide license, if that's what you mean," said the proprietor. "But he's the best damn fisherman in the entire county, maybe the whole state. Why do you think we call him Fishboy?"

"You mean you're just offering to take me out for fun?" I asked Fishboy.

"Yeah, but maybe I'd let you pay for the gas." He shrugged. "You understand what *a'm* sayin'?"

"I think so."

First we had to go back to Fishboy's place to collect his boat. Fishboy lived in a house he'd built himself back in the woods. He was a part-time carpenter and handyman and it was a good solid, tidy house, by no means the rough-planked hermit's shack that I had sort of expected—though Fishboy was clearly a bit of a hermit. But the most extraordinary thing about the house was the inside—every square inch of wall space was covered with

mounted fish and game. Wall after vast wall—a shrine to the sporting life, a veritable game museum. It took my breath away.

The entire living room and kitchen were devoted to bass, "368 of them," Fishboy said proudly as I walked around dumbstruck, "88 of them over ten pounds."

"Wow," was all I could think to say.

Fishboy admitted that he had designed and built the house largely to accommodate his collection of mounts. There was something both touching and a little sad about it, not to mention deeply eccentric.

Several other rooms were devoted to ungulates—mounted heads and walls of racks—whitetail deer, mule deer, antelope, elk. "I went out west last year," Fishboy said. "During bow season. I never hunted elk before, but I read everything about it I could get my hands on." He told me where he had gone, and oddly, it wasn't that far from where I lived in Colorado; I knew the area well—I also knew bow hunters who had been hunting there for years and had yet to kill an elk or, for that matter, even get off a shot.

"How did you do?" I asked.

"I got a six-point bull on the first morning," he said. "So then I had to trout-fish for the rest of the week. I'd never caught a trout before." He named a river with which I was familiar, one that I have fished many times over the years.

"How'd you do trout-fishing?" I asked again.

He pointed to a huge brown trout mounted on the wall. "Just under six pounds. Caught it on the fly-only stretch. First time I ever fly-fished."

I neglected to mention that I'd been fly-fishing all my life and had fished that same stretch of river for upward of fifteen years and had never even seen a fish that size.

Then there was a room full of game birds—quail and pheasants, turkeys, and several species of grouse, ducks, and geese.

"All these mounts must have cost you a fortune," I said.

"I did most of them myself," he answered. "Sent away for a mail-order taxidermy course."

"They're damn good," I said. "It must have taken you hundreds, thousands of hours."

"A'm getting better at it all the time, and faster. . . . Course, I get a lot of practice. You understand what a'm sayin'?"

"Perfectly," I said. "I'll bet it doesn't leave much room for a social life."

"Well, I had a date just last week," Fishboy replied a bit defensively. "Took her to the movies and then I brought her back to see my house." He looked momentarily puzzled, a bit hurt. "She didn't much care for the place. Said it gave her the creeps. You understand what a'm sayin'?"

"Sure, I can see where a first date might not get it," I said. "Listen, Fishboy, this is none of my business, but how do you have time to make a living if you fish and hunt all the time?"

"Well, I don't really," he admitted. "I used to work full-time for a contractor, but I like to make my own schedule and now I work private jobs just long enough to get a little money together so I can hunt and fish more. I love to hunt and fish; that's all I think about. It's all I ever wanted to do, ever since I was a kid. I'm just tore down by it. You understand what a'm sayin'?"

"I think I do."

Later that morning we were floating on a southern river that will remain unnamed, through a forest in rolling hill country that put me oddly in mind of a western landscape. The river ran through hills of red sand-clay, through vast stands of longleaf pines alternating with loblolly pines and hardwood, through stands of spruce pine and white cedar and cypress along the riverbanks; there were mixed stands of magnolias, their leaves dark green and waxy, their flowers white and fragrant, red maples

and sweet gum, slash pines and ash. The wild azaleas were in bloom, the redbud and yellow jessamines flowering.

The water was dark, blacker than any western river, but pure and sweet, and the sandbars and small beaches carved along the turns were as white as sugar. We would float silently for a time through dense cypress swamps, casting bass plugs up against the undergrowth. Then suddenly we would break out into an open floodplain, where spring wildflowers bloomed in the sun. Turtles basked on logs in the river, slipping softly and nearly soundlessly into the water if we came too close, and a couple of times we saw the periscopelike eyes of submerged alligators watching us from up against the bank.

The bass were not "*hawgs*" by any definition, but there were plenty of them, and they hit our topwater plugs with loud swirling sounds that punctuated the quiet like small underwater implosions. They were beautiful, healthy fish in this pristine river environment—glistening mottled black along their backs, graduating to deep greens and pale olives, their bellies white and their gills bloodred.

Toward lunchtime we put in at a small clearing along the bank, cleaned a few fish, and fried the fillets in a cast-iron skillet over a propane stove. Rolled in cornmeal and fried in bacon grease and served with corn bread, the bass were almost unimaginably sweet and delicious.

While we ate, Fishboy filled me in on the flora and fauna hereabouts. He was as knowledgeable as, probably more so than, any wildlife biologist, and he knew the countryside like his own living room—which, in a real sense, it was, for this was where he lived most of the time.

"I never buy meat or chicken at the market," he said. "Just don't care for the taste of it. Why eat domestic animals when you can eat wild ones? You understand what *a'm* sayin'? And I save a lot of money that way, too. About all I ever have to buy is staples—cornmeal, flour, butter, lard, salt. I eat what I kill

and I only kill what I'll eat. I trade fish and game to a local colored lady for produce in season—so I get all the greens I need—and I do some canning. I catch all the bass and bream I can eat. I shoot ducks—good wood duck shooting out here on the river in the fall; I'll take you sometime—and sometimes I'll drive down south to the marsh and shoot snipe. I love them damn little snipe, the way they zig and zag. Good eatin', too. Plenty of turkey around, and quail, deer, wild hogs. My, but I do love wild pig! Especially where they been eating acorns. And then, like I told you, I try to make a trip out west every fall—drive straight through, thirty hours nonstop—bring home a truckload of elk and mule deer meat. I killed a bear one time in the forest not too far from where we are right now; this was when they still had a season here on black bear—you understand what *a'm* sayin'?—but to tell you the truth, I did not care overly much for the taste of that bear meat, and I never killed another one after that. Too many other good things to eat in the woods to bother with bear meat, you understand what *a'm* sayin'?"

It occurred to me that Fishboy was living the life that boys once dreamed of—or at least that I once dreamed of when I was a boy. It was a kind of Daniel Boone/Davy Crockett fantasy, the notion of Huck Finn lighting out for the territory, living off the land, on intimate terms with wild country and wild creatures. I wondered if boys still dream of these things or if their dream lives have been largely taken over by video games and virtual reality, by television and movies, by professional sports stars and action heroes.

However, nostalgia for childhood dreams is a dangerous and largely unproductive indulgence. As I watched this rather strange and gifted man, Fishboy, that day on the river, I also wondered if there isn't sometimes a trade-off for those so obsessed with the sporting life—the more comfortably a man fits into the natural world, often the less well he is able to accommodate himself to civilization. Of course, some people move

quite comfortably between both worlds, while others, like Fishboy, were clearly awkward in what we think of as the "real" world. Perhaps, like Dean Wavrunek, the mountain man whom I had met in Minnesota, Fishboy had simply been born in the wrong century, when the skills of hunting and gathering and basic survival are so much less applicable to our lives. There was a time when a woman might have looked upon him as a real catch, rather than simply an oddity. Married to him she would never have wanted for food on the table or animal hides to keep her warm, and presumably she would recognize that his offspring, too, would be genetically endowed with these useful life skills.

Now we were back on the river after lunch, floating and lazily casting our bass plugs up against the bank. The spring birds were singing from the undergrowth, the insects making their cacophony of junglelike sounds, and yet it was still and silent, if you know what I mean—just the sounds of the river as we drifted by, without a care in the world, leaving not a trace of our passing.

"You ever get lonely out here?" I asked Fishboy.

Fishboy thought about the question for a while. He considered it so intently that I wondered if it had ever occurred to him before. "No, I can't say as I ever get lonely out here," he finally answered. "Not when *a'm* fishing and hunting, because then *a'm* doing something I love, you understand what *a'm* sayin'? *A'm* thinking so hard about it, concentrating 100 percent." He paused and looked thoughtful again, a bit troubled.

"But sometimes after I get home late at night, when all the lights are out and the house is dark . . . yes, sometimes then I do get a little lonesome . . . you understand what *a'm* sayin'?"

23

JUST FOR THE FUN OF IT

It was early morning and I was fishing with my friend Jimbo Meador from Point Clear, Alabama. We had run over the border to the Florida panhandle to fish the flats around Santa Rosa Sound, Grand Lagoon, and Pensacola Bay for speckled trout and redfish. Then we thought we might run out into the gulf and look for mackerel and cobia.

Meador is a lanky, slow-speaking Alabama boy who grew up in Mobile Bay and has been poking around these parts all his life. A boyhood friend of author Winston Groom, Jimbo was one of the models for the original fictional character Forrest Gump—with the important distinction that Jimbo's not slow.

Presently Jimbo was trying on a new fly of his own creation—a possum fur fly that he tied himself from a possum that his Catahoula leopard dog, Clyde, caught and killed in the yard. "You know, that's kind of a strange thing," Jimbo said, holding up the fly. "I trimmed a little fur off that possum to make this fly and then I double-bagged him and put him in the bottom of my chest freezer. I planned to just cut fur when I needed it for

flies, and when I'd used it all up I'd throw the body away. The next day, I went into the freezer to get something out and damned if that possum wasn't sitting up on the top shelf. Course, by then he was frozen solid. The poor damn thing hadn't been dead after all. Somehow he managed to crawl out of both bags and up on that shelf." Jimbo shook his head sadly. *"Daaaamn,"* he said in his deep, distinctive drawl, "I felt just *terrible* about that." Then he smiled slyly. "But I guess that'll teach him not to play possum."

The day before, we had taken a short boat ride from Jimbo's house on the bay up into the delta, the rich, watery country where Jimbo spent his youth. Back then he'd cut school for days, weeks at a time, so that he could indulge his passion for duck hunting, alone and free to explore, to learn all he could about the birds and the animals, the fish and the tides. I envy him the knowledge he has gained by living in such a place as this all his life, the kind of knowledge that seeps into your bones from an early age and is so difficult, if not downright impossible, to acquire later in life.

Now Jimbo was poling me around a rocky point where he knew a school of redfish hung out. I was standing up in the bow trying to spot them. Earlier as we were planing out here at dawn over the flat steel gray surface of the lagoon, the sand dunes and spits of land had flown past like half-formed thoughts. These coastal regions with their bays, estuaries, deltas, sounds, lagoons, flats, and points are just a different kind of country, defined by water in the same way that desert is defined by lack thereof, and hunting up this resident school of redfish was not unlike working a familiar covert for a covey of quail.

"There they are," Jimbo said, pointing."See 'em? About two o'clock? Get ready!"

But infuriatingly, I did not see the fish in time, I flubbed the cast, lining the school, and the first really good look I got at the redfish was of them scattering through the water like a burst of Fourth of July fireworks. Polite, as always, Jimbo said nothing.

Now he ran us out into the gulf to the edge of the tide line where the water went instantly from murky to a crystalline blue-green and where terns wheeled, fluttered, and dived with stabbing precision into schools of bait fish while ungainly pelicans plunged indelicately, but no less successfully, into the sea, coming back up to flip their heads back and drop fish down their gullets like workingmen knocking back shots at the bar.

A squadron of Blue Angels from the nearby naval base in Pensacola flew low over our boat in perfect formation, and a giant seaplane with some sort of sensor that looked like a flying saucer mounted on its bottom lumbered heavily by, scanning the ocean for who knows what purpose.

This set me to wondering if maybe both the natural world and the taxpayers might not be better served if the government simply sought out low-tech people on the ground like Jimbo here, people who understand and, as important, love the country in a familial sense—sons and daughters of the earth. I have found these people everywhere, in every small town in every region of America that has not been completely paved over—people who have been listening and watching and learning all their lives, who know how to hunt and fish and survive outdoors. They know instinctively how to husband their game. They know the names, habits, and habitat requirements of the fish, birds, and mammals—not only the game species, but the nongame as well, the indicator species, the predators and the prey.

We anchored over an old wreck, and Jimbo had me cast into a tight pod of bait fish, a huge, writhing brown ball, like a single organism, big as a Volkswagen—even I couldn't miss that cast. With safety in numbers, the bait fish each aspired to be at the center of the ball, the larger fish picking them off the edges and the birds diving on them from above. A school of mackerel entered the scene like a fleet of heat-seeking missiles, attacking the bait pod with gusto until it seemed to literally explode. And the big fish ate the little fish, as we would eat the big fish.

Later that afternoon we ran back in to check out another of Jimbo's favorite trout and redfish spots. As we were dead-drifting across the flat, an enormous manta ray the size of the boat ghosted past. Then Jimbo pointed in the air and I looked up to see four pelicans spiraling above, gaining altitude with each pass, riding the thermals until they were nothing more than specks against the sky. "Why do you think they do that, Jimbo?" I asked.

Jimbo considered the question, looking up at the circling pelicans, nearly out of sight now. "Well," he said, nodding thoughtfully, "I think they do it just for the fun of it."

24

THE LAST WILD COUNTRY

Nobody knew where this man come from, and nobody asked him. You didn't ask a man hard questions, not in the Ten Thousand Islands, not in them days. Folks will tell you different today, but back then there wasn't too many in our section that wasn't kind of unpopular someplace else. With all of Florida to choose from, who else would come to these overflowed rain-rotted islands with not enough high ground to build a outhouse, and so many skeeters plaguing you in the bad summers you thought you'd took the wrong turn straight to Hell.
> —Peter Matthiessen, *Killing Mr. Watson*

Let's say that you've never caught a tarpon on a fly rod before and that presently you're standing in the bow of a skiff, in a small, secluded bay deep in the dark, mysterious maze of mangroves, bights, bays, creeks, and rivers that comprise the Ten Thousand Islands on the southwestern coast of the Florida Everglades. It is raining steadily, has been raining since you left the dock in Chokoloskee well over an hour ago, and already

you're soaked to the bone. But you've forgotten about the rain for the moment, about any sense of personal discomfort, because the tarpon are rolling lazily on the surface in the bay all around you, flashing silver in the dingy, overcast early-morning light, and making a deep, sonorous suction sound that seems vaguely familiar. You tap your reservoir of fishing memories and realize that the sound resembles that of big trout feeding on a still lake at dawn, only this particular sound is amplified and deepened a hundred fold, as though played through the best stereo system on earth, with the bass turned way up. And now the odd thought occurs to you that the fish you're about to cast to with this pitifully flimsy wand of a fly rod is roughly the same size as your wife.

You cast out ahead of the wake, let your fly sink a moment, and start a slow, steady retrieve. When the take comes there is no mistaking it, nothing remotely delicate about the throbbing *boom-boom* that vibrates all the way up into your shoulders and down to the tip of your toes. You make a sharp, final, hopefully hook-setting strip and raise your rod tip, and the fish, unaware even that it is hooked, simply keeps swimming steadily. You may as well have hooked onto the back end of a tractor. You set the hook again, twice, hard, pumping your rod with everything you've got, which only serves to inform the tarpon that it is, in fact, hooked, at which point it starts swimming in earnest. Now rather than being hooked to a tractor, you have the even more helpless sensation of having your fly attached to the bumper of a Ferrari; line burns ferociously off the reel. You'd like maybe to try to put the brakes on somehow, but as if astride a runaway horse with no reins, you have no idea how to slow the damn thing.

Then suddenly the tarpon decelerates on its own, slows, and stops in one of those odd momentary lulls that promises something of great import in your immediate future. And here it comes; the tarpon breaks the surface, 100-plus pounds coming straight up out of water like a shuttle launch, shaking and twisting, and when it lands again it is with the sound of a piano hitting the water. And then suddenly it's over, your line slack,

your heart sliding back down your throat to your chest where it belongs, your hands trembling as you wonder, *Did that really happen, or was it just the greatest fishing wet dream I've ever had?*

For those who mourn the loss of the "old Florida," it is heartening to note that you won't find any trace of Mickey and Goofy in this part of Florida. It has always been wild country, and folks have always come here to hide out, to disappear in this strange, watery, mosquito-infested land—barely land at that, most of it less than a foot above sea level.

The ancient Calusa Indians were the region's first inhabitants, taking up residence approximately two thousand years ago. Were it not for their efforts there wouldn't be enough high ground on Chokoloskee Island for human habitation; they built up the shell mound that keeps the island mostly above sea level, even in hurricanes—135 acres and 25 feet high in places—an engineering feat that represents a good deal of shucking over the centuries.

Credited with killing Ponce de León in the early 1500s, quite possibly right here in Chokoloskee, the Calusas seem to have vanished from the region by the mid-1700s, probably victim to European diseases imported by the Spanish.

The Seminoles came next, pushed down to the heel of Florida in the course of three extended wars with the United States, their original population of 5,000 souls winnowed down to a remnant 100 or so. This last handful were able to effectively elude their U.S. Army pursuers in the impenetrable labyrinth of mangrove islands, creeks, and tidal rivers. They never surrendered, never signed a peace treaty with the government—the only Native American tribe to have managed this decidedly Pyrrhic victory. Some of their ancestors still inhabit these parts.

After that it was mostly men on the lam from other states and other regions who filtered down here to get lost: escaped slaves, convicts, hermits, and eccentrics. It was good country to hide out in. Who would follow them here, and if so, who could

ever find them? Men like Ed Watson, who showed up in Chokoloskee around 1892 and was rumored to have killed the woman outlaw Belle Starr out west. During the years that Watson farmed on the Chatham River, a number of his acquaintances and employees mysteriously disappeared or turned up dead until he was himself finally gunned down by vigilante neighbors on October 24, 1910. In fact, as you motor out from the Chokoloskee dock in the morning you'll pass the old Smallwood store where they killed Mr. Watson.

Then there was the hermit plume hunter and fisherman old Juan Gomez, of Portuguese descent, who claimed to have met

Napoléon as a boy and to have sailed the high seas with the pirate Gasparilla. Believed to be the oldest man in the United States, Gomez drowned, tangled in his anchor line, in 1900 off Panther Key at 122 years of age.

And a man named Guy Bradley, one of the original game wardens for the Audubon Society. Around the turn of the century plumes from egrets, roseate spoonbills, great blue herons, ibis, and other wading bird species native to the Everglades were a popular fashion statement on women's hats. In New York, egret plumes sold for as much as thirty-two dollars an ounce, literally more valuable than gold at the time. During the spring, when the birds were in full plumage and had nestlings to tend and so were especially vulnerable to the hunter's gun, thousands were slaughtered in the rookeries for their feathers, their carcasses left to rot, their young to starve in the nest or to be picked off by buzzards.

By 1901 wading bird populations in the once-prolific rookeries of the Ten Thousand Islands had been so decimated that the state of Florida outlawed plume hunting. Guy Bradley was assigned this territory to patrol against poachers. On July 8, 1905, he tried to arrest a former Confederate Army captain named Walker Smith and his sons, who had a boatload of illegal egrets and cormorants. Smith shot and killed Bradley, who thus became the first Audubon warden to die in the line of duty—a chilling echo from the past in view of our own present-day game wars.

Here are no lofty peaks seeking the sky, no mighty glaciers or rushing streams wearing away the uplifted land. Here is land, tranquil in its quiet beauty, serving not as the source of water but as the last receiver of it. To its natural abundance we owe the spectacular plant and animal life that distinguishes this place from all others in the country.

> —Pres. Harry S Truman, address at dedication of Everglades National Park

You are poling the edge of a bight near the mouth of Lostmans River, casting to a grass line up against the mangroves. This is the transition zone, where rivers meet the sea, where freshwater mingles with salt, the fecundity and variety of life palpable in the rich, pungent smells and the wild sounds of the mangrove forest.

Earlier up Lostmans River you saw alligators cruising the shoreline, and at the mouth of the river you watched a plump manatee grazing placidly in the shallows. In the flats of the bay a blacktip shark cruised past the boat.

Now the rain has finally abated, the tide is falling, and the roseate spoonbills are congregating in the mangroves patiently waiting for the mudflat to be exposed: dinnertime, a smorgasbord of delicacies. They are garishly dressed creatures in full breeding plumage—bright pink with brilliant crimson shoulder and neck patches, saffron-colored tails, red legs, black ear patches, bare, greenish heads with red eyes, and spoon-shaped bills—who manage to be both beautiful and goofy-looking at the same time. Bait fish skitter all across the still gray surface, pushed up against the mangroves by larger fish. A school of dolphin work through the bight, arcing gracefully from the still water to bust shiners with calm deliberation.

From back in the flooded mangroves come the resonant tones of snook feeding, a heavy popping sound like bricks being lobbed into the water. As the tide falls, the snook come out to feed on the edge. You wait for them.

As you drift silently by, bald eagle nestlings watch from their perch on the edge of their nests, waiting for Mom and Dad to bring home some chow. Prior to fledging they are actually larger than the adult bird—they haven't flown yet to burn off all that baby fat.

Wood storks and ibis, snowy egrets and great blue herons wade the sandbars and flats, feeding with perfect precision. The food chain is a magnificent thing to behold, and you are part of it.

You throw your popper up along the grass, right on top of a

fresh snook swirl, and retrieve it like a bass popper—*ballumpf,* let it sit, *ballumpf,* let it sit, *ballumpf* . . .

We never had no time for sport, we was too busy living along, fighting the skeeters. In the Islands we worked from dawn till dark, just to get by. Didn't hardly know what sport might be till we all got hired out as sport-fish guides and hunters. This was some years later, after the fish and game was gone for good.
—*Killing Mr. Watson*

Even your guide, a man named Capt. Robert Collins, is in a sense a modern-day refugee from the "real" world, hiding out down here. He grew up in Miami, went to school in Coral Gables, and now will barely go back there, even to visit his parents. It's gotten too crazy, he says. Collins lives in Naples and fishes the park all year in all seasons and knows it intimately, knows where the tarpon cruise and where they lay up, knows where giant schools of redfish gather in passes or tail in shallow bays, knows where the snook hang along mangrove shorelines or up against a long line of beach. You have made a wise choice, a good investment; even experienced Glades rats can get lost in the maze of the Ten Thousand Islands, and it would be insanity to try to explore and fish it the first time without benefit of a guide.

Fishing the morning tide in a bay up Lostmans River, you jumped three tarpon in a hour, but none were brought to the boat. This is not uncommon, due to the hard cartilage of their mouths, and it's just fine with you. On a fly rod, especially for a novice to tarpon fishing, it can take an hour or more to land a big fish and they will often fight to the death. In any case, the real fun of it is in the take, the first few spectacular jumps, a long screaming run or two. As Captain Collins pointed out, had you brought the first one to the boat, you wouldn't have had the chance to jump the other two, as the tide would have turned in the time it took to land it.

Then you ran out and fished the beach line for snook and redfish. And then into the mangrove bight. . . . You've been rained on and, when you tried to explore the shore for a few minutes, chased back to the boat by a cloud of saltwater mosquitoes, even more aggressive and voracious than their freshwater cousins. And you have seen more diversity of wildlife in one day than you see in most months.

Clearly, the Everglades are not dead yet. Threatened, to be sure, diminished, yes, but not dead. Far from it. And what you have learned for sure is that there's plenty here still worth saving.

Maybe game warden Guy Bradley's tragic death was not entirely in vain, for with protection the plume birds made a remarkable comeback between 1901 and the 1930s. Sadly, since then the Glades have been vastly reduced in size; six-sevenths of the historic Everglades lies outside the 1.5-million-acre Everglades National Park, which alone among our national parks has been named an International Biosphere Reserve, World Heritage Site, and wetland of international importance.

Endless water projects to feed the insatiable South Florida development juggernaut and the politically powerful, heavily subsidized sugar and dairy industries have drained, canaled, and leveed the "river of grass" that once flowed in a sheet from Lake Okeechobee to the gulf. Inconsistent water levels, ill-timed releases, and pollutants in the form of mercury and nutrient-enriched agricultural runoff have resulted in a 93 percent decline in the number of wading birds nesting in the rookeries of the southern Everglades—down from 265,000 in the 1930s to just 18,500 today.

The endangered Florida panther, which, like the remnant Seminoles, is making its last stand here, is thought to number fewer than thirty animals statewide. A panther with mercury levels that would be toxic to human beings was found dead recently in the park. This, too, is the last home of the American crocodile, a species that lives in the salty, brackish waters of the transition zone. Also endangered, the crocodile has lost so much

of its natural habitat that only a dozen active nests have been identified in the park.

The Everglades is a national treasure, a paradise, a watery wilderness without parallel on earth, and we may allow ourselves to feel slightly encouraged by recent massive efforts on the part of private and public agencies and individuals to restore and protect it. These include a large land acquisition purchase/swap between the state of Florida, the federal government, and the sugar and dairy industries, which, feeling the scorching heat of public opinion turned upon them, are trying to reinvent themselves as conscientious land stewards—a spin-marketing feat of no small magnitude. Clearly, sportsmen have as much to win or to lose in the battle for the heart and soul of the Everglades as anyone else.

Now you are running back in at the end of the day, bouncing lightly over the choppy water of the bay. Overhead a rare Everglades kite flies by holding an apple snail in its talons. A moment later an osprey wings heavily past, carrying a large mullet. Sure, so maybe you're not bearing a fish of your own. So what? It's enough just to know that these wild creatures have made their living here today. And you hope they will tomorrow, too.

25

LA VIE

Manger, manger, manger, manger
Travailler, travailler, travailler, travailler
Lutter, lutter, lutter, lutter,
Rire, pleurer, rire, pleurer,
Dormir, baiser, baiser, dormir,
Jouir et souffrir, souffrir, souffrir,
Aimer, hair—aimer, hair,
....

et chier
Manger, manger, manger, manger
Travailler, travailler, travailler, travailler
Lutter, lutter, lutter, lutter,
Rire, pleurer, rire, pleurer,
Dormir, baiser, baiser, dormir,
Jouir et souffrir, souffrir, souffrir,
Aimer, hair—aimer, hair,
....

prier

....

—Mourir—

—Count Pierre de Fleurieu, "La Vie,"

English Translation:

Life

Eat, eat, eat, eat
Work, work, work, work
Struggle, struggle, struggle, struggle
Laugh, cry, laugh, cry
Sleep, fuck, fuck, sleep
Play and suffer, suffer, suffer,
Love, hate—love, hate,

....

and shit
Eat, eat, eat, eat
Work, work, work, work
Struggle, struggle, struggle, struggle
Laugh, cry, laugh, cry
Sleep, fuck, fuck, sleep
Play and suffer, suffer, suffer,
Love, hate—love, hate,

....

pray

....

—Die—

CATALOGING IN PUBLICATION 10/99

Fergus, Jim.

The sporting road : travels across America in an airstream trailer, with fly rod, shotgun, and a yellow lab named Sweetzer / Jim Fergus. — 1st ed. — New York : St. Martin's Press, 1999.

p.   cm.

ISBN 0-312-24245-X

1. Hunting—United States.   2. Fishing—United States.   I. Title.

SK41.F4   1999

799'.0973—dc21

99-15930

AACR 2   MARC CIP 10/99

Perhaps some of you will remember my old friend the count. I'm afraid that a number of readers have confused him over the years with another of my friends, and it is true that it's a confusing matter, and one largely of my own making. I have intentionally obfuscated things to the point that even I've become confused on the subject. But to set the record straight once and for all: this count of whom I speak here was a different person altogether than my other friend. I say "was" because this count passed away recently, peacefully in his sleep. As I hadn't seen much of him in the past few years, I am grateful to have had the opportunity to spend a few days on his farm last spring shortly before his death.

I was struck then by the fact that the Count had aged a bit. Don't get me wrong, he still seemed fit as a fiddle, but gaunter than I remembered him, and though his memory for stories of the old days was as keen as ever and his considerable gifts as a raconteur still much in evidence, I noticed that he seemed somehow less *engagé*, as the French say—that is, less committed to this world. Not that the Count had ever had the slightest interest whatsoever in current events or popular culture; in fact, I don't think he'd ever even read a newspaper. Since he'd left his native France decades ago he had tended to isolate and insulate himself, creating his own perfect version of the world on his farm—the general location of which I am forbidden to mention in print, even now that he is dead.

Regardless of what time of year it was, when I went to visit the Count he would always insist upon organizing sporting expeditions for me. He was very old-world about that. If it was fall or winter, he organized dove shoots for my entertainment or got me invited on exclusive quail hunts on the plantations of his neighbors. In the spring and summer he would line me up to fish with various local "characters." Sometimes the Count accompanied me on these expeditions; other times he sent me off on my own.

In this particular case, which would prove to be the last time that I was to see the Count alive, he had arranged a bass-fishing outing on a nearby lake and had decided to come along with me; and truly, I hadn't seen him this excited about a fishing trip in a long time.

Our guide was a young local fellow named Ennis Tartt, and the Count assured me that today I was going to see bass fishing like I'd never seen it before.

I should just mention that for as long as I'd known the Count, going on thirty years, he'd always been kind of a purist, even a bit of a snob, when it came to fishing. A serious and expert practitioner of the art of fly fishing, the Count had fly-fished all over the world—he'd caught everything on a fly from salmon in Iceland to sailfish off Costa Rica; he'd done it all. In fact, some years ago he published a book of stories about his fly-fishing adventures. *Fly Fishing Around the World*, it was titled, long since out of print, though the few copies in existence have become quite valuable as collector's items.

Well, you can just imagine my surprise when the Count announced to me that Ennis Tartt was the best bait fisherman in the entire state and that we were going to be bass-fishing with live shiners. *"Live shiners?"* I asked, dumbstruck. "C'mon, Count. You—a man who has turned his nose down at bait fishermen for years—are going to bass-fish with *live shiners?"*

The Count's narrow, hawkish face crinkled up in childlike delight, and he beamed mischievously. "It's terrific fun!" he assured me as if he'd just discovered a new and slightly naughty recreation.

So then we were at the dock, loading our gear into Ennis Tartt's bass boat. Actually, Ennis was supplying most of the gear, because the Count didn't own any bait-casting equipment. Soon we were planing across the lake to one of Ennis's favorite hot spots, where we anchored and he sprang into action.

Although he's not a professional guide, he wouldn't let us do

anything on our own. In fact, we were barely allowed to touch the rods until Ennis gave us permission. He had six—yep, count 'em—six casting rods rigged up with hooks and cork floats.

A fit, tan, blond, bearded man with plenty of energy, Ennis scurried about the boat like a dozen busy mates, fishing live shiners from his bait well, neatly skewering them onto hooks, and heaving the lines out until they ringed the boat in a full circle—three rods laid down over the gunwales at both our feet. Personally, I prefer to hold a rod in hand, but as I say, Ennis didn't allow this—and for the obvious reason that a bass might just as easily hit one of the other baits and then you'd be holding the wrong rod. Nevertheless, with all those lines out, it seemed to me that if a big bass hit and started fighting in earnest we were in for a terrible train wreck of a tangle. But what did I know about it? In fact, I wasn't even sure which float out there belonged to which rod. There is an art to live shiner fishing, and clearly it was going to take me a while to get the hang of it.

The strikes started coming almost immediately. Sometimes there would be some warning. For instance, a particularly energetic—and frightened—shiner might start swimming for all it was worth, towing the float like a tiny water-skier, which of course, suggested that something, hopefully a large bass, was chasing the shiner. The first time this happened, I grabbed the rod in question (at least I thought it was the rod in question) and struck like a rank beginner. This was absolutely the wrong thing to do. First of all, it was the wrong rod. Second, as I was soon to learn from Ennis—who had grabbed the right rod, while cussing me up and down like a marine drill sergeant—you're supposed to wait, allowing the line to free-spool as the bass picks up the bait, swims off with it, and then finally stops to eat it at its leisure. If you make the mistake of striking too soon, you rip the bait right out of the fish's mouth.

Now at the appropriate moment, Ennis handed me the rod.

"Go ahead and hit it," he said. "I mean really knock the shit out of it!"

Well, this kind of fishing may not be everybody's cup of tea, but I can tell you that I'd never seen the Count so happy. He sat up in his chair in the stern of the boat, surrounded by his rods, giggling like a kid at the city park on Huck Finn Day, while Ennis scurried adeptly between the rods, cussing and re-baiting and casting and checking lines and handing us rods to strike—all the while issuing instructions as the bass took our shiners. We struck and sometimes hooked them and just as often missed, which angler error would unleash from Ennis yet another string of epithets: "Goddamn, son of a bitch, you missed him! What did I tell you? You gotta *hit* the son of a bitch! *Hit* him!" he would holler. He meant no harm; he only wanted so badly for us to catch fish.

And the Count was truly having the time of his life. He would be all wide-eyed when the float went under and would pick up the rod and strike for all he was worth, and even if he missed, especially if he missed, he would start to giggle, and his narrow face would get all pinched up in delight until tears ran down his cheeks, and once he got to laughing so hard that he actually began drooling.

You know, one great common denominator, whether we are rich or poor, royalty or commoner, American or otherwise, is that in a real sense we all begin our angling careers as bait fishermen. And I think maybe this whole experience reminded the Count of when he was a boy, before he became an expert fly fisherman, a purist, when he used to fish with bait in the moat that surrounded his ancestral castle in France. In his prime the Count had caught as many fish and as many different species on a fly rod as any man in the world. Who was to deny him this final boyish fun?

Now that I think about it, that's when I first knew that the Count wouldn't be with us much longer, that he was slipping away into his childhood. And that is the image I'll forever after

carry of him in my mind's eye: sitting up in the bow of that bass boat, face pinched up in an expression of the purest wonder and delight, like a young boy on his first fishing trip, giggling until tears ran down his face.

26

TURKEY MADNESS

The story the locals tell in Trinidad, Colorado, is that shortly after Frenchman Marc Jung purchased his 50,000-plus-acre ranch outside town he caught a poacher hunting on his property. Jung stuck the business end of a .357 Magnum in the poacher's ear, drove him to the nearby Holiday Inn off the interstate, and marched him into the lobby, where, in front of astonished staff and guests, Jung phoned the local gendarmes to report the crime. Well, it's how things are done in France, where poaching is simply not tolerated. Actually, Jung felt that his response was quite measured. Back home he might just have shot the poacher.

There were two important facts, however, that Monsieur Jung had not taken into account: First, in America the law frowns on those who pull loaded guns on others—even to apprehend a poacher on one's own property. And second, the poacher was the sheriff's nephew.

However, after the legal and judicial dust had settled, fines had been paid, and appropriate amends made, Marc Jung had a

name (already in use by the natives) for his spacious new spread: the Crazy French Ranch.

Crazy like a fox, maybe; by all accounts poaching incidents are down on the Crazy French.

"I thought we'd take a little drive around the ranch this evening," suggested outfitter Butch Whitten, a lean, long-legged, long-armed, loose-limbed, six-foot-five man in cowboy boots and bell-bottom jeans (and I don't mean boot-cut jeans; I mean old-style bell-bottoms). "Show you a little of the country and see if we can't spot a turkey or two."

I don't know, maybe there was some cheap irony to be found in the fact that we had come to Trinidad, Colorado, the sex-change capital of America (no kidding), to impersonate hens. It was April and we were here to hunt the wild gobblers on the Crazy French Ranch with Whitten. I'd been hearing "Butch Whitten" stories from my friend (and Whitten's neighbor) Doug Baer, who had put this hunt together, for so long that I was beginning to think that Whitten might be a figment of Baer's imagination—a kind of alter ego. I figured if even half of these stories were true (and I know now that they're all true) this was a man who had lived more lives than the big cats he hunts, had more adventures than most outdoor writers make up in their whole careers.

Here's one: One time Whitten was guiding a rich man on a cougar hunt. His dogs, Treeing Walker hounds, were hot on the trail of a big cat, Butch loping behind them; in those days it was nothing for him to run twelve to fifteen miles a day, day after day, behind his dogs. The dogs finally got the cat pinned in a shallow cave, really no more than a little overhanging depression in the rock, and by the time Butch caught up to them two of the dogs had already been nearly mauled to death trying to go in after the cat. Butch got the dogs tied up as best he could and was trying to minister to the wounded when his assistant, alerted by walkie-talkie, arrived with the client. "There's your cat," Butch said to the man. "Go ahead and shoot him."

"No, I want him treed," demanded the client. "I want to take pictures of him in a tree before I shoot him."

Whitten is from the old school of outfitters; if the asshole wanted his cat in the tree, well, OK. . . . However, the big cat had different ideas on the subject; he felt secure in the cave and had no intention of coming out.

So Butch had his assistant distract the cat with a stick while he reached in and grabbed the animal by the tail and pulled him out of the cave. When Whitten let go the cat ran, and the dogs took up the chase again and finally treed him. The client got his photographs.

A former rodeo bull rider, turned race car mechanic, turned law enforcement officer, turned federal undercover agent (Whitten worked for the Department of Interior in its antipoaching division but quit after four years, "because some of the people I was working for were worse than the people I was setting up"), Butch Whitten is one of the world's great trackers of men and animals and about the toughest son of a bitch (no offense meant toward your mom, Butch) that you'd ever want to meet.

Of course, Whitten has also been a renowned big-game outfitter for most of his life (his father was an outfitter and government trapper in northern New Mexico for forty-seven years), with a special reputation as a mountain lion and bear hunter. Butch has guided and hunted with the greats, the near-greats, and those who just think they're great. (He once even guided the legendary outdoor writer Jack O'Connor on a bighorn sheep hunt toward the end of his life, when the alcoholic old man could do nothing but hang around camp all day smoking cigarettes and drinking. O'Connor later claimed in a magazine article he wrote about the trip that he had shot a sheep actually killed by another member of the party.)

"So what's with the bell-bottoms, Butch?" I know this might seem like a strange question to ask a man like Whitten on a first meeting, but I had to know. "I haven't seen pants like that since the Bee Gees."

"Yessir," Whitten answered, nodding, "I'm down to my last two pairs. I wear them because I can get my knife out of my boot fast. You can't do that with the boot cut."

"Yeah, well, I had a hunch it wasn't a fashion statement."

Besides me and Doug Baer, rounding out our group were Steve Collector and Backland Camouflage president and designer Scott Anderson, a world-class turkey hunter in his own right. We all squeezed into Butch's extended-cab Ford pickup and headed for the ranch.

Set in the transitional zone between mountains and plains, and between the central Rockies and the Southwest, the Crazy French Ranch occupies a substantial chunk of southern Colorado, hard against the state of New Mexico. This is a rugged hilly border land of piñon pine, spruce, juniper, cedar, and scrub oak. The country is both rough and magnificent, rimmed by rock escarpments that fall away to heavily timbered slopes that give way to brushy creek drainages that open up into hidden valleys and meadows.

The ranch is as rich with history as it is with game. Long before it belonged to the Frenchman and was part of Colorado, it belonged to the Spanish and was part of Mexico; long before it was part of any state or country, it belonged to the Jicarilla Apaches. And long before that, the Anasazi called it home.

The current tenants have done a superb job of managing the land for wildlife. Avid hunters and dedicated conservationists, Marc and his wife, Evelyn Jung, chose the legend "*Priority for Wildlife*" as the Crazy French Ranch motto. Enrolled in Colorado's "Ranching for Wildlife" program, whereby 40 percent of the hunting licenses issued to the ranch go to the public (available through a lottery system), the Crazy French is a true wildlife haven. The Jungs have strategically placed irrigated food plots all over the property—grain and alfalfa crops and grass meadows that they do not harvest or graze but grow strictly to feed the

wild animals. Although they run some cattle on another part of the ranch and raise bison on yet another, in three days of turkey hunting we would not see a cow on the place or any sign of one—a rare luxury indeed on a large ranch in Colorado. We would see elk, deer, and fresh bear signs and even make one very rare breathtakingly close-up sighting of a mountain lion. And we would see plenty of turkeys. I mean to say, *plenty* of turkeys.

Whitten stopped the truck on the winding ranch road that rises up out of the canyon bottom. He walked in front of the vehicle, listened attentively for a minute, and then, using his box call, gave one short, seductive call. A tom answered almost immediately, his deep gobble resonating off the hillsides as if in an amphitheater.

Butch walked the turkey strut back to the truck, his head bobbing sinuously on his long neck, his long legs rubbery. No man ever looked more like a turkey. He climbed in the truck. "We might have a turkey or two on the place," he deadpanned.

We drove up the hillside, through a series of gently rising switchbacks, as Whitten and Anderson engaged in an arcane conversation about turkey calling—pro to pro. "No two hens sound the same," Butch said, so as not to leave us laymen out of the loop. "I've heard a old hen sounded like the worst man-made call you ever heard. Sounded like my ex-wife, God rest her soul—if she's not dead."

We crested a small rise and dropped down into one of the irrigated food plots where at least a dozen turkeys were feeding, among them several big toms. "Yessir, we may have a turkey or two on the place," Whitten repeated, nodding. He stopped the truck and we all got out quietly while Butch made his music on the box call; he was answered by a big old gobbler, who fanned his tail and danced the turkey trot, pirouetting and strutting as if purely for our entertainment.

I have to admit that this was the first strutting gobbler I'd

ever laid eyes on. "Wow! Look at the size of those damn birds," was all I could think to say.

"Not exactly quail, are they?" Collector said.

"More like ostriches," I replied in awe.

The turkeys had spotted us by now and were melting into the trees in the dusk along the edge of the field. We climbed back in the truck and drove up the other side of the draw to a kind of plateau from which we were afforded a spectacular panoramic view of the countryside all the way across to the San Juan Mountains due west, the high peaks still capped with snow, the Sangre de Cristos to the north and east. In the middle distance the twin Spanish Peaks rose in nearly perfect symmetry, lifting 7,000 feet above the plains. "The Indians called those mountains the Breasts of the Earth," Butch said. And you could see why.

"Well, I'm sportin' a wood," confessed Anderson, who gets pretty excited when he sees turkeys.

"It's all the testosterone flowing this time of year," Collector observed. "Men are hopeless."

Way before dawn the next morning, way before dawn, we were sitting in the starkly lit Bob & Earl's Cafe next door to the motel, eating one of those hunter's breakfasts that turn your arteries to stone, while plotting our strategy.

The writer kills the first bird, that's the rule. At least that's how Butch wanted it, and who was I to second-guess Butch Whitten?

I'm not much of a "morning person," but if you have to be up before dawn, you may as well be sitting at first light with your back against a tree, in the middle of a copse of mixed scrub oak, juniper, and pine, in full camo and face mask, listening to the rich gabble of turkey talk all around you. Last year's brown fall leaves were still on the ground, green shoots of grass poking

through, the buds on the trees just beginning to swell. A squirrel went about its business, now our business, running up Butch's arm to gain the tree trunk behind us.

Butch worked his box call. Of course, as in duck and goose hunting, the true challenge of hunting turkeys lies not in pulling the trigger after someone else has done all the real work for you. In any case, the kill itself is an anticlimax, and I had already made up my mind that although I could not pass up the rare opportunity to do this the first time with a true pro, I would not kill another turkey until I had learned the art of calling myself.

I didn't need to know much about it to know that Whitten is a master. He has big gnarled hands, scarred and crooked from years of bar fights and up-close-and-personal encounters with cats and bears and murderous poachers, and yet the soft and plaintive sounds that he makes on his box call are the turkey equivalent of those of a Stradivarius played by a concert violinist.

Butch had not one but three toms responding to his calls; he was the most popular hen in the woods this morning, all the fellas coming in to meet him. "He's double-gobbling," Butch whispered to me of the bird that was clearly the front-runner. "He's hot; he's comin'." If the tom's testosterone was flowing, so was my adrenaline.

And then there he was, coming up over a little rise ahead of us, just as planned, winding through the trees, tail fanned, head bobbing, prancing and twirling for the ladies. Of course, he had no way of knowing that it was to be his last dance. He seemed in no great hurry to meet the new hen, wanted first to strut his stuff for her. But come he did, and Butch whispered, "Take him whenever you're ready."

"When I started out hunting as a kid," Butch said, "I basically had all of northern New Mexico to hunt." The sun was rising, lighting first the rocky plateau above us, a high butte formation where it was easy to imagine the Anasazi hanging out, and then

flooding the saddle beneath the rimrock, before spilling down the brushy draw. "Now just about everything that I used to make a good living at," he continued, "is either illegal or considered to be immoral. This country is thick with cats, and now that the spring bear hunt has been banned in Colorado there's an overpopulation of bears that's going to cause real problems down the road. When the cats kill a few more joggers and the bears eat a few more campers, maybe then the bunny huggers will get the idea . . . but I doubt it."

We had loaded back up and were moving to another spot to set up again. I was finished with my own hunt thirty minutes after daybreak on the first day, my trophy a two-year-old twenty-two pound Merriam with an eight-and-a-half-inch beard. The Frenchman's rule is one man/one bird, and that was fine by me. Now I had the rest of the weekend to watch the others, to see the country, and to pick Butch Whitten's brain.

As we drove, Butch entertained us with tales of undercover poaching operations: "I got myself thrown in jail for a week in the Yucatán as part of a sting I was setting up," he said. "There was seventy-six men in my cell and I was the only Anglo." He grew suddenly pensive. "You know," he continued in a lower voice, "a lot of guys think they're tough, but you put 'em in jail in old Mexico and they'll find out how tough they are."

He told us tales of famous people he has guided, including a number of professional baseball players: "They have a lot of fun in camp," he said, smiling. "They're just like kids who never had to grow up."

He told us about prominent political figures caught poaching and crooked game wardens and sundry government intrigues. Butch plays by the rules and by an unimpeachable code of personal honor that seems sadly anachronistic in this day.

He told us stories about his old man, who died a few years ago at eighty-seven years of age, and about one particularly Gestapo-like ex–game warden in his area, a longtime nemesis whom Butch hasn't had to whup yet only because "my dad

whupped his ass when he [Butch's dad] was seventy-eight years old. And then my kid whupped his ass."

Hearty stock, these Whitten men.

He told us stories about hunts and adventures from Mexico to Alaska.

"You ever hunted in Africa, Butch?" someone asked.

"Nosir, I have not," he answered. "I don't believe I'll ever make it to Africa."

"No interest in going there?"

"I won't lie to you," Butch said. "I'd fight a grizzly bear with a toothbrush, but I had a few bad experiences in airplanes when I was working undercover and I'm deathly afraid of flying."

A goshawk got out of a tree on the side of the road like a spirit and flew a tricky slalom course through the woods. We crested a rise and dropped down the other side; every bend in the road and every peak seemed to reveal a new mystery. Deer browsed on the edge of a meadow and two elk trotted across the far side. Another herd of turkeys grazed.

Dawn the next morning: violent wing flapping and a crashing of branches in the woods announce a trio of hens getting up off their night roost and sailing into the field; they glide in with wings set in the dawn's first light, big as B-52s, making an audible *whooshing* noise and then back-flapping for landing, dropping their feet and touching down with surprising grace for such enormous birds. They lower their heads and begin feeding, making their soft *putt-putt* sounds.

Doug Baer and Scott Anderson are set up on the edge of the field. Whereas Butch Whitten uses one or two basic calls to bring the gobblers to him, Anderson, who is a kind of camo design savant, has more calls in his arsenal than Jim Carrey has facial expressions; Scott has box calls and mouth calls and slate calls, with which he can sound like anything from an owl, to a hen, to a tom turkey, to a goose (yes, even a goose; don't ask

me why). Too, Anderson tends to move more than Whitten, calling and repositioning—he's a strategist with a full bag of tricks. Different styles, both effective.

Now Scott begins a long romantic conversation with an ardent tom, whose deep warbling gobbles echo out of the shadowed timbers, seeming to fill the whole world in the specific still of daybreak.

"It's like God made that bird to make that noise to make spring beautiful," Anderson whispers in a reverent tone.

"And to drive us crazy," adds Baer.

But the tom will not come. We had all worked this bird the day before; he's big and he's smart, he's seen us around, and he's on to us. He will not come.

The hunters reposition themselves; the tom follows, comes closer, hangs up. The same sequence repeats itself. The romantic negotiations continue, Scott imploring the tom to come in to meet him, face-to-face, a real date, the tom answering, *It's springtime, I'm hot to trot, I'd love to add you to my harem, but you'll have to come to me.*

The hunters capitulate; now they are following the tom, the way proper hens should. He leads them on an obstacle course through the woods. Anderson is the turkey expert, but this is Baer's country and he knows his way around. They make a good team. Periodically they stop and Scott calls to the tom and several times the bird comes back, gobbling, approaches well within killing range, but the forest is too thick now to allow a clean head shot. Half a dozen times, both Scott and Doug begin mounting their guns only to drop them again as the tom fades back into the forest: *Come along, ladies.* They follow.

Now Scott and Doug are sliding on their butts down a steep embankment, looking at each other, grinning like kids. Now they are running downhill, trying to get around on the other side of the tom. They are like a pair of wild creatures themselves now, primitive, pure predators, focused, the hunting gene kicking in like an afterburner to fulfill this one mission. The ground

levels off at the base; the hunters circle to either side, each always aware of the other's position, Scott still calling; the gobbler answering.

Finally the bird steps out of the cover into a small clearing, revealing himself to Scott; it's the first and last mistake he'll ever make in the timeless dance of predator and prey.

Later, as the hunters recount the hunt, re-creating it step by step, Scott says to Doug, "I really wanted you to kill that bird, but I had to take the shot when I had it."

"Oh, hey," says Doug, "it was good for me, too."

Scott's bird turns out to be a different species than mine, a Rio Grande turkey, quite rare in this area, which is on the very northernmost edge of their range.

"I talked to my girlfriend last night," Whitten said. "She was in a real good mood because she found $350 with her metal detector in the backyard. It was buried in a Gerber baby food jar."

OK, I'll bite: "Why is there money buried in your backyard, Butch?"

"My father buried money all over the place," Whitten said. "After the depression he never really trusted banks again, so he cached his money. My girlfriend's up to about four thousand dollars so far, just that she's found in the yard."

A cold front was moving into the region, preceded by high winds that came up that afternoon, the worst possible weather conditions for hunting turkeys. We went out anyway; only Doug Baer had yet to kill his bird—pure circumstance. Now the wind was gusting thirty to fifty mph and everything seemed askew in the world. The turkeys weren't in their usual haunts, and the toms weren't gobbling. Romance was clearly not on their minds, and who could blame them?

Butch, carrying decoys, and Doug, carrying a shotgun, were walking abreast down a fire road; Collector brought up the rear,

carrying his cumbersome load of camera equipment. Suddenly Doug and Butch spotted an animal moving off the road ahead.

The shadows seemed to give the animal's hair a reddish cast and at first Doug thought it might be a fox, but it was far too big to be a fox. "Butch, what is that?" he whispered.

"Cougar," Butch answered.

In the wind the mountain lion had evidently neither heard nor smelled the hunters approach, and she saw them about the same time they spotted her. She was in a small opening, exposed, and just as a house cat will do in a similar situation she crouched and froze and looked right at them, no more than thirty feet away. Later Butch would tell us that though he has hunted mountain lions for some forty-odd years and has either killed or been in on the kill of better than one hundred of them, he's only ever walked up on six in his life. Now the cat (a young one-hundred-pound female, Butch later estimated from her track) began to slink off, her belly nearly dragging, a sinuous crawling motion that broke into a low-to-the-ground run. The men watched her away for 300 yards.

The hunters continued down the road, where they set up. Shortly thereafter, Butch called in a tom and Doug killed the bird. Butch figured the young lioness had been stalking the same bird: Two of the most efficient predators on earth pursuing one of the wiliest prey; it was just that turkey's day to die.

SUMMER

27

CATCHING DINNER

"In our family there was no clear line between religion and fly fishing," begins Norman Maclean's classic work, *A River Runs Through It.*

I know just what he means: when I was fifteen years old my father took me on a road trip from our home outside Chicago to the venerable Orvis store in Manchester, Vermont. It was the beginning of summer vacation, 1965, and we drove across the country, just the two of us, in a Ford Countrysquire station wagon, stopping well before dark each night to camp. At the Orvis store Pop bought me an Orvis "99" bamboo fly rod, a low-end model no longer in production, but to a young boy back then, the finest fly rod on earth. After that we bummed around New England, camping out and fly fishing on some of the storied rivers: the Battenkill, the Ausable, the Beaverkill.

My father was not a rich man but he tried to show me new water and new fishing experiences every year. We always drove on these expeditions. Over the years of my childhood we cast plugs for northern pike in Wisconsin, plastic worms for large-

mouth bass in Texas, popping bugs for brim in Lousiana, trolled ballyhoo for sailfish in Florida, and flipped dry flies to trout in Wyoming. We fished worms and minnows and grasshoppers, for everything from perch in Lake Michigan to King Mackerel in the Gulf Stream. We were generalists.

But the year we toured New England and I got my Orvis fly rod was the year I became a true devotee to the religion of fly fishing—and specifically of fly fishing for trout. It seemed to me to be the culmination of my short angling career, the ultimate fishing experience. Maybe I remember it so well because it was the last fishing trip Pop and I ever took together. He got sick and died less than a year later. But he had lived long enough to instill in me a love of the road and of all these varied forms of fishing—some of which I am just now rediscovering.

Thirty years later, I'm still on the road, still bumming around and still fishing. But not long ago, I realized that somewhere along the way I had lost touch with my fishing roots. I had become a terrible fly fishing snob; I now looked down my nose at those who used spinning or casting rods. As for the lowly bait fisherman, well, in my book a bait fisherman was himself just one step above a worm on the evolutionary scale.

More recently a kind of curious reversal has begun to take place in my fishing sensibilities. Ever since the movie version of Maclean's novel came out, it seems like every urbanite in America has taken up fly fishing. The western trout rivers that I have known and loved and fished for three decades are suddenly choked with nouveau anglers sporting spandex and neoprene, flogging the water with graphite and mylar, talking on cell phones to their offices in New York and Los Angeles from the river's bank for God's sake. Suddenly a big, fat nightcrawler begins to seem somehow more natural. Yes, I've been thinking of renouncing my faith in the religion of fly fishing.

One early June morning not too long ago, I found myself in a flats boat in a bay on the Florida gulf with my friends Father Valdoni, a retired priest who presides over a gaggle of Carmelite

nuns, and Tommy Robinson, a fishing guide/realtor who works out of Apalachicola. It is another sign of the times these days that many former laid-back fishing guides have become more high-powered fishing guides/realtors. Now, not only can they take you out fishing but they can also sell you your dream property in paradise.

Anyway, "Dad" (as Tommy and I call the priest, no disrespect intended) and I were fishing, while Tommy, the junior among us, was poling the boat. We were fishing for redfish, casting shiny gold spoons up against a grassy shoreline. Tommy had brought along a variety of equipment—including both fly rods and spinning rods—and he had given us our choice. With only a bit over an hour to fish, both of us, somewhat shamefacedly, as if we were committing a deadly sin, chose the spinning rods.

"These days I just like to feel the fish pulling," Dad said in a slightly apologetic explanation of his choice of rods.

"Yeah, me too," I admitted.

Truthfully, it'd been a long time since I'd cast an open-faced spinning reel with any regularity, and on my first attempt I forgot to open the bale. I flung my spoon around in a short arc and damned near hooked the good father in the nose. "Whoops, sorry Dad!" I said.

"Not to worry my son," he said. "Possibly God is thinking of punishing us for forsaking the fly rod."

The father got a hit almost immediately. He missed it, but on the next strike he hooked and landed a nice redfish. It was a couple of inches over the minimum legal length—perfect eating size.

"You want to keep that fish, Dad?" Tommy asked.

"I'd love to have it for my dinner," Dad said. Spin fishing and killing a fish to eat—a second mortal sin to the new religious order of fly "fisherpeople."

"Well, it is Friday," I pointed out. Even though I'm not Catholic we were accomplices now, fellow fishing sinners.

Dad caught, hooked, and landed another redfish. "Dear Lord,

I love to feel them pulling!" he said. "Shall we keep this one for your dinner, my son?" he asked me.

"Thanks, Dad," I said, smiling, "But I can catch my own dinner."

"Well, I'd take one," Tommy said.

After a while, I finally got the hang of the spinning rod again. I loved the way it was capable of hurling the spoon so far out and the way the spoon arced in the air and landed with the solid *ker-plunk* that has warmed many a young boys' hearts.

Pretty soon, I hooked a redfish. I liked the way it pulled, too, and in short order I brought it to the boat. Best of all, I liked that I had caught my dinner.

Please don't misunderstand me: In a crowded world with ever more pressure on our natural resources, including our fisheries, I am a firm believer in, and a steadfast practitioner of catch-and-release angling. I've been releasing most of my fish since I was ten years old—long before it became fashionable. But there are still some places and circumstances in which it's alright to kill a fish or two for dinner. In this same way, there are certain waters and species whose bounty and fecundity can support, within sensible limitations, the perfectly natural process of human predation. As much as I still love to do it, as much as I think it is appropriate to many species and waters, I no longer think of fly fishing as a religion.

We had fished for only an hour or so but it had been one of those rare perfect outings in which everyone had a fish to take home for dinner. Now it was time to go in; we all had other things to do and we were all going our separate ways. Tommy ran us back across the choppy bay. The father closed his eyes, either snoozing or praying. I was thinking about Pop.

28

TRUE SPORT

The sun has just broken the horizon, flooding the bay with red-tinted light. The birds are on the move, terns and gulls, pelicans and ducks, moving low across the sky, occasionally breaking formation, wheeling and diving, plunging into the still water to stab bait fish. Mullet jump in their goofy cartoonlike way, launching themselves from the water and sailing horizontally through the air before belly-flopping inelegantly. One flies directly over the bow of my kayak like a trained porpoise. As we glide silently up on an exposed sandspit, a bald eagle lifts off, no more than twenty yards away, the breadth of his wingspan astonishing at such close range.

No roar of engine, no diesel fumes, no wake, with just the slightest whisper of paddles cutting water, we slip up on an osprey elegantly picking a snake out of the marsh grass. Seeming to recognize our benign intentions, she barely flinches at our presence and swallows her meal with leisurely relish.

The redfish, too, seem unaware of our approach; they feed up

in the grass, flooded at high tide, the hump of their backs exposed as they wriggle through the mud in the shallow water like creatures trying to crawl from the sea in an evolutionary tale.

It is this ability to enter the natural world, to literally slide into it so unobtrusively that is one of the great pleasures of kayaking, and by extension fishing from kayaks and the kayaker is granted access into the domain of fish and wildlife as if we still inhabited their world in some meaningful, primal way. Offering more intimate contact than even a canoe, the thin shell of the kayak is like an extension of our own bodies, allowing us to feel the water beneath us, the currents and tides, as if we are not so much passengers but a part of the element itself.

I am fishing in Apalachicola Bay with my friend Richard Bickel, a professional photographer, who introduced me to the sport of kayak fishing and who is such an aficionado of it that he'll never go back to conventional water crafts. "The last time I fished from a power boat," he says, "I felt like I was fishing out of a car window."

Never is the sense of closeness to the element more immediate than when a fourteen-foot alligator (whose populations are growing in the region) slips off the bank in front of us. "Ah, Richard . . ." I say as the gator glides to a halt ten yards ahead, snout and eyes exposed. Our kayaks drift to a stop, too, facing the gator as if in some kind of surreal showdown at sunup.

"I think they're just curious," Richard says. "I've never had trouble with them. But you know what my local friend George says?"

"No, what does George say?" I ask, without taking my eyes off the gator.

"George says, 'Richard, you're *crazy* to go out in that thing,'" says Bickel, adopting a local panhandle drawl. "Why to them big gators, you're just like an oyster on a cracker!"

As if on cue the alligator sounds, just sinks beneath the surface like a waterlogged piece of driftwood.

For the sake of simplicity, Bickel fishes primarily a close-faced spincast reel sometimes casting a weedless spoon into the grass but often simply drifting across the flats in a tidal current, trailing a line with a shrimp on a hook and little or no weight. Entirely self-educated about both kayaks and angling, his low-impact point of view has not only taught him a great deal about the indigenous wildlife of the area, but he also catches a lot of fish—depending on the season and where he chooses to go: redfish, speckled trout, flounder, striped bass—most of which he releases. And whereas fishing with shrimp might seem unsporting to some, the way Bickel does it—his kayak floating on the currents like a piece of driftwood, the shrimp flowing along in the tide like a dead-drifting nymph in a trout stream—is about as natural as you can get.

"Every now and then one of these bassmaster guys who ride around in $30,000 boats with twin 135-hp Evinrudes will give me a hard time about fishing with bait," he says. "I just tell them that I'd like to see their fat ass in a kayak sometime. That usually shuts them up."

I am fishing with a fly rod today—a minor complication of Richard's minimalist ethic—and though you might think that casting a fly from a kayak would be problematic, it is actually surprisingly manageable. Sea kayaks are wider-hulled and infinitely more stable than river kayaks, or most canoes for that matter, and it is really no more difficult casting from them than it would be if you were wading up to your waist in a river. Better yet, the newer sit-on-top models are so stable that a well-balanced (and preferably, experienced) fly caster can actually stand atop them to cast. (Hey, I didn't say that *I* could do it.)

As the tide turns and the sun clears the horizon, we paddle out to fish the oyster bar, our kayaks slipping soundlessly over the skinny water, another great advantage to a kayak being that

it allows the angler to reach places inaccessible by other fishing craft—all you need is a scant few inches of water.

Here the fish cruise the edge where the oyster bar drops off to deeper water and is shallow enough that sometimes we even get out of our shells, tether them to our belts with a short line, and wade up and down the bar casting, the kayaks following behind like faithful dogs.

The oystermen, too, have taken up their positions along the bar this morning; silhouetted against the rising sun they stand atop the platforms of their flimsy low-slung plywood boats, dipping their tongs into the water and lifting huge dripping basketfuls of shellfish.

We drift across the bar on a falling tide, and paddle back to drift it again. I am casting a gold-spoon fly, an odd, but effective imitation of a spinning lure. In the very shallow water I can feel it bumping along the shell bottom and when it stops I think for a moment that I'm hung up. But when I lift the rod, I feel the unmistakable life of the fish in the tuning-fork vibrations of the tip, and as the line straightens and the rod arcs, the kayak swings around to face it. Then the oddest thing happens: the fish begins to tow me, the kayak acting as drag. I feel a little like Santiago in Hemingway's *The Old Man and the Sea*.

Richard laughs. "Hey Jim," he calls to me. "See you later! It looks like that fish is going to take you on a little tour of the bay!"

29

THE RITES OF SUMMER

We have no spring to speak of in the high country where we live; the weather goes from winter to summer and back again. I was driving, as I often do, from Florida to Colorado in early June watching the country greening up as I went. I had dozens of different routes to choose from; when you've made the trip as often as I have it becomes a challenge to avoid repeating one-self—which is also a good discipline for columnists.

The intensely verdant South was already humid and dense, in full summer flower. I stopped for the night in a campground outside Gulfport, Mississippi, where I purchased and consumed several pounds of raw oysters, sprinkled with horseradish and hot sauce and washed down with longneck Dixie beers. Next to me was parked a van, trailering a boat, with a fellow's name stenciled on it in large letters and beneath his name the legend: "*Musician *Entertainer *Ventriloquist *Magician *Fishing Guide *AND TRAVELING MINISTRY." This sort of thing seems specific to the South. (I know, for instance, a bunch of

western fishing guides, and not one of them doubles as a minister and magician.)

Early the next dew-soaked morning while preparing the Airstream for departure I happened to meet the owner of the van, and I briefly toyed with the idea of hiring him for a half-day of fishing. But I changed my mind when he tried to introduce me to his ventriloquist dummy.

"Do you accept the Lord Jesus Christ as the only true Savior?" asked the dummy right off. (He looked astonishingly like the fallen evangelist Jim Bakker.)

But I could clearly see the man's lips moving, and I couldn't help but wonder what his magic act must be like. "I'm afraid you're wasting your time," I answered. "I'm a practicing Zen Buddhist." I'm not really, but I began to chant anyway. Sometimes you have to fight fire with fire. Don't get me wrong; I have nothing against religion or, for that matter, entertainment, but I prefer my fishing unencumbered.

The South gave way gradually to the big West Texas landscape that always made me feel that I was nearing home again. Just outside Memphis, Texas, I had to brake hard to avoid running into a flock of wild turkeys, ambling across the road like a bunch of truant school kids.

This year I decided to cut up through the Oklahoma panhandle and into Kansas, across the plains that seem so briefly fertile this time of year, especially in a wet year such as this one. Then I struck the Arkansas River bottom and followed it on into eastern Colorado, where I caught my first glimpse of the mountains on the western horizon.

It was down in the river bottoms that summer was most in evidence, with the cottonwoods in full leaf and the black-soiled floodplain, now mostly in farm crops, green as at no other time of year. The ducks and geese were on the move, the air above the river filled with their traffic.

Every year I worried that I would miss the beginning of sum-

mer at home when I saw how far along the season was in the flatlands. And every year I arrived too early, leaving summer behind as I climbed the mountain passes, always surprised to see that, far from having missed the season, it hadn't even begun in the high country yet. Often it snowed in early June and the mountain peaks were almost always still white. At 8,600-feet elevation, our mountain park was usually barely greening up yet, the willows in the creek bottom and the aspens in our yard just beginning to leaf out.

The fall before I had to put down my old Australian shepherd, Caddy, and I had buried her on the hillside above the garden. She had been with me since I first moved up to this cabin fifteen years ago. She was my fishing dog—the main requirement for which being that they not get in the way. Sweetz has always been a lousy fishing dog because she always wants to be hunting out in front, which is just where you don't want them to be.

So one of the first things I did when I got home was go over and kneel on Caddy's grave and pat the large river rock I put there as her headstone, and I spoke a few words to her, for I still missed her, as we do all our dead dogs for the rest of our own days.

Then there was the matter of the small ritual that Caddy and I performed every year while preparing the garden for planting: catching and eating the first trout of the summer.

The creek behind our house was still muddy and swollen with runoff; it would be weeks before it or any of our other trout streams were ready to fish with a fly. So I dug up a fat worm in the garden and impaled it on a hook attached to a length of line with some splitshot a foot or so above the bait. Then I tossed the worm into the back-eddy of a deep pool where the river oxbowed and where I knew a trout always lay. I tied the other end of the line to a willow branch. When Caddy was alive she would sit on the bank watching the trotline intently while I worked in the garden. She'd sit there for hours, and when the

line started to twitch she'd bark to warn me and I'd climb over the garden fence and haul in a fat brown trout to cook up that night for dinner.

Of course, this year with Caddy gone it wouldn't be the same. Still, it was a summer ritual and so I went through the motions, digging my worm, rigging my trotline—just for old times' sake, in memory of Caddy more than anything else.

I was working up a pretty good sweat in the garden and I'd nearly forgotten all about my trotline when, an hour or so later, I thought I heard a dog barking on the creek bank. I paused in my work and leaned on the shovel and listened harder. There it was again. I swear it was Caddy's bark, the echo of her bark, like a perfect memory. I looked over at Sweetz, who in typical off-season Lab fashion had been dozing in the sun on the deck. She had raised her head and was listening with ears cocked forward; she heard it, too. Then I remembered the trotline and I looked over at the willow branch. It was twitching and bobbing and dancing like a witcher's rod.

Thank you, Caddy, my good old girl, my fishing dog. Rest in peace.

30

SHOOTING SCHOOL

Look; I've humiliated myself with a shotgun in front of some of the great wing-shots in America, so when I first step up to the shooter's station at the famed Holland & Holland Shooting Grounds in the verdant English countryside outside London, chief instructor Ken Davies at my elbow, I have no great expectations. All I'm really hoping for is not to break the spell. A quiet, elegant, somewhat lepraunchish-looking fellow with thick blondish gray hair, beard, and nattily twirled mustache, dressed in tweed "breeks" (breeches), a tattersal shirt, and wool hunting-scene necktie, Davies seems almost like a cliché, a character playing the role of nineteenth-century British shooting instructor in a *Masterpiece Theatre* presentation. This is the first bona fide shooting lesson I've ever taken in my life. I've come all the way to London for it, and maybe it's the jet lag, but I have the distinctly odd sense that as soon as I pull the trigger, thereby betraying the full range of my own vulgar, graceless late-twentieth-century American shooting style, I will shatter the illusion altogether; I fear that I'll wake up back at the town

dump at home, where I practice my shooting with my rancher friend Billy Cantrell.

"Consider me to be the worst wing shot in America," I warn Davies, who has been teaching here for twenty-seven years and is widely regarded as the premier shooting instructor in the world.

"Let's have a look, then, shall we?" says Davies, blowing his whistle for the first clay bird.

As if to prove my point, I promptly miss the first five targets, a pitifully easy going-away warm-up shot that even I ordinarily break. "Jet lag?" I offer by way of lame excuse. (I have hundreds of them.)

Davies considers me with twinkling eye, strokes his beard thoughtfully, and finally shakes his head. "Gun mount, I'm afraid."

I'll be the first to admit it: nobody needs shooting school more than this shooter. Though a relatively proficient athlete all my life, I came to the art of shotgunning late and with an astonishing and frustrating maladroitness. Finally exhausted by my own ineptitude, tired of embarrassing myself in the field in front of my many expert shooting friends and of disappointing my dog with repeated misses, I decided to take matters in hand.

So it is that in my quest to nail down once and for all the fundamentals of proper shotgunning technique, I went right to the source—Holland & Holland Shooting School, quite possibly the most venerable (they've been teaching the art of shotgunning since before the turn of the century) shooting instruction program in the world. In the space of a few weeks I would be coached by some of the world's most accomplished instructors, both British and American; I would fire nearly two thousand shotgun shells, during which time, as a result of my habitually (possibly pathologically) poor gun-mounting technique, the outside of my shoulder would bruise to resemble an overripe egg-

plant. A seemingly permanent lump of scar tissue would form on my jawline from same poor gun mount. The inside of my thumb where I flicked the safety on and off a couple of thousand times would be lacerated like a raw carrot passed across a grater. And my brain, from all that concentrated instructional input, would, as one of my favorite H & H American instructors, Gil Ash of Houston, Texas, puts it, "turn to mashed potatoes."

———————

Early June, and it is snowing at the Vail Rod and Gun Club, (host to the Holland & Holland Sporting Clays Week,) whose clubhouse and sporting clays course are perched in the sage-and-juniper foothills outside Walcott, Colorado, some twenty miles west of the famous ski town. The temperature hovers just above freezing as I step up for my first turn at the first station of the day. The instructor is Chrissie Alexander-Davis, British Ladies champion from 1977 to 1990, before retiring from competition, to be coached by Ken Davies in the art of teaching. The bird is a high incomer ("passing goose") off the snow-dusted rocks on top of the hill above—a long, falling floater that gives the shooter rather too much time to think things over. But I patiently watch it, mount slowly and smoothly, and dust this first bird of the week. (A good omen perhaps?) "Lovely," says Chrissie. Lovely! Ah, the magic of a clean, well-taken shot! But on the very next target, my dicey gun mount (which involves ratcheting the gun up to my shoulder with my right arm, rather than smoothly extending it out toward the target with the left) begins to reassert itself. Still, I manage to break the bird and turn hopefully for another precious word of praise from my instructor. "Well, you killed the bird," she says, frowning, "but it wasn't pretty."

"Don't worry, *dahlink*," consoles Austrian bombshell Sheika Gramshammer. "I have trouble with my gun mount, too." Sheika, one of the instructors' favorite students, is taking the course for the second year in a row. She and her husband, Pepi, run the Gasthof Gramshammer in Vail, which, along with the Sonnenalp, provides lodging for the shooters. "My boobs are too big! They get in the *vey* of the gun!"

A sense of camaraderie quickly develops among the students, encouraged by the realization the very first day that somebody here shoots much like you do, and for much the same reasons.

There are experts and rank beginners, serious sporting clays competitive shooters here to fine-tune their skills and dedicated bird hunters taking the course as a means of improving their wing-shooting. There are a handful of participants, primarily the bird hunters among us, carrying side-by-side doubles, while the vast majority of participants are shooting over-and-unders, many of them sporting clays competition guns.

There is even a general and bona fide American hero in attendance—Norman Schwartzkopf (an excellent shot in his own right). And Michael McIntosh, the stylish shooter and renowned shotgun writer, is also here.

My own group on opening day provides a kind of socioeconomic, geographic, and sporting microcosm of the participants at large: one accomplished shooter—a duck hunter and timber baron from Michigan named Randy; one average shooter, Mike, an upland bird hunter and commercial pilot who hails from Boulder, Colorado; one relative novice, Liz, an heiress from Palm Beach, here primarily because of her husband's interest in shooting; one complete beginner, a young man from the Netherlands by the name of Oswald, whose father, the Dutch ambassador in Washington, is also taking the class. And, of course, yours truly.

American instructor Gil Ash (winner of a number of shooting titles including the twenty-gauge National Sporting Clays Championship) mans the next station—"fur and feather," a rabbit target bouncing along the ground, followed by a crossing aerial shot. Ash is a dancing, jaunty, roly-poly, energetic, in-your-face style of instructor who puts great emphasis on the visual aspects of shooting. He is currently explaining to me why both my footwork and my eye focus are hopelessly messed up. "Listen to me!" he says, waving his teacher's aid, a tiny plastic replica of a clay pigeon, in front of my face. "*Listen* to me! Now look, bubba. You don't mind if I call you bubba, do you? First

of all, you didn't really see the target, did you? Did you see the spot in the center of the target?"

"Ah, no, I guess not," I admit sheepishly.

"No, you *didn't*," concurs Ash. "But I really think a lot of your problem is your footwork. The way you've positioned your feet in relation to where you want to break the target—it doesn't work. Trust me on this. You're making things way too hard for yourself. You know, it'd be like trying to pick your friend's nose while you're jogging." (I love this little guy; he really gets me looking at the target, and all week long I will shoot well at his station.)

By our third station—"crossing woodies"—our duck hunter, Randy from Michigan, is already in trouble, beginning to delaminate from instructional overload. (And still only the first day!) Meanwhile, our beginner, Ossie of the Netherlands, is coming on strong; he offers a clean canvas to the instructors, with no bad habits to correct or any counter productive shooting "attitudes." Liz from Palm Beach is gaining confidence, and Mike and I, with our double guns and common interest in flushing dogs, are already fast friends and planning a hunt together in the fall.

American Dan Carlisle—Olympic medal winner, twenty times national champion, a gonzo, serious shooter, and impassioned type-A instructor—works this station. Carlisle, who emphasizes the visual and the mental aspects of shooting, as well as precise timing, teaches a method he calls the "pull-away" system, whereby the shooter "inserts" his barrels in front of the bird and pulls away from it, thereby, in theory at least, never getting behind the target.

But Randy, a hunter rather than a target shooter, is having difficulty grasping the concept: "Would you mind if I just did it my own way?" he finally snaps in frustration.

"Not at all," says Carlisle agreeably. "You go right ahead, *pardner*." Randy misses half a dozen more birds in a row. "We

can stand out here all day long," Carlisle finally observes, "and you're never going to break a bird that way."

"How can you talk to me like that?" demands the now-outraged, red-faced duck hunter. As a rich person, Randy is unaccustomed to being criticized.

"Because I've missed more targets than you've ever shot at in your life," explains Carlisle with perfect equanimity. And in another minute he has the now-defused duck hunter breaking clays.

Next station, "flaring mallards," coming from behind and overhead, the instructor Jon Hollinger, an outfitter and bird hunter from Aspen. Hollinger is the only nonprofessional instructor and the weakest of the lot, his specialty the ergonomics of gun fit; he quickly decides that my stock is too short for me and adds a slip-on pad.

But at the very next station debonair British instructor Roland Wild, a former farmer and himself an avid game shooter (who beat out 120 applicants to fill "dead man's shoes"—a single coveted opening in the Holland & Holland instructional team), removes the pad (gun fit, without a formal fitting, being a subjective art form). "I think it's interfering with your gun mount," Roland explains. Trained by Ken Davies, Wild, too, is a relaxed, quiet, easygoing instructor.

By the time I get to our last American instructor, Jerry Meyer, who is working the "sneaky snipe" station, a quick going-away shot, I am beginning to experience a bit of overload myself; I'm thinking too much, tight as a wound spring, my gun mount jerkier than ever. Meyer is the instructor's instructor, author of the *The Sporting Clays Handbook* and *The Clay Target Handbook*. Inspired in the Holland & Holland method several years ago when he watched Ken Davies's video, *Game Shooting*, Meyer teaches a "gospel according to Jerry" with all the fervor of a Southern Baptist preacher.

"Kid, you need to relax," Meyer says to me. "You're too tense;

you're seesawing your gun up to your shoulder with your right arm. Extend your left arm out toward the target. Give me your gun for a minute. Watch how I extend with my left arm." Nothing cheers the student more than watching the teacher miss a target with your gun, and at one time or another throughout the week I would see almost all of the instructors miss birds while demonstrating proper technique (which only serves to demonstrate that even the best shooters are mortal). But in this case, as if to prove that there is nothing wrong after all with a gun that stubbornly refuses to break targets for me, Jerry immediately breaks several in a row, and then, as if he has magically retrained my gun in the process, I break a few. ("I healed the kid!" Meyer boasts.)

And finally, the incomparable Ken Davies at the "sitting duck" station—an aptly named looping, following double—preposterously easy slow-moving targets. Except I can't for the life of me hit them. Davies, wearing his Sherlock Holmes hat today, is still concerned about my gun mount, which remains recalcitrantly low on my face; I simply seem unable to get the stock up to the fleshy part of my cheek.

"It's because my boobs are too big!" I explain in my best Tyrolean accent.

"That's Sheika's excuse, Jim," Davies says.

So it goes more or less all week: the participants divided into different groups each day, each instructor working a different station—intensive though never tiresome instruction, over two hundred shells fired every day by each student. Although instruction is standardized under the rubric of the "Holland & Holland method," if there is any potential pitfall to the program it is simply in having "too many cooks," each with a slightly different teaching technique, the cumulative effect of which can be to give the student too much to think about. (For my part, I have plenty of things to work on: my gun mount is all wrong,

my footwork sucks; I have sloppy eye focus, poor concentration; I'm too tight, not fluid enough; my gun doesn't fit me.) If the Brits tend to be soft-spoken shooting stylists, concentrating on butter-smooth gun mounts and elegant body motion, the Americans tend to be aggressive technicians, teaching the nuts-and-bolts mechanics of target shooting with born-again fervor.

Witness British instructor Chrissie Alexander-Davis, stylishly attired in a dark green corduroy English shooting vest, telling Gen. Norman Schwartzkopf that she would like to see him looking more "balletic" when he shoots.

"You want me to look like a ballerina?" laughs the general. But Schwartzkopf is a fine athlete, who came by his nickname "the Bear" not only for his size but also for his smooth, rolling, bearlike gait, and in no time he's wielding his gun with downright balletic grace.

"That's lovely! Much better!" says the pleased instructor. "I'd rather have you miss the bird and look good than kill it and look bad."

And at the very next station Gil Ash, dressed in running shoes and lightweight pastel slacks, is not about to let the general get away with an unsatisfactory gun hold point. "Listen to me!" Ash says in his inimitable fashion, waving his miniature target and hopping about in front of the general. "*Listen* to me! Target analyzation!"

"Jeez, I'm being harassed by a guy in pink pants," remarks Schwartzkopf.

Speaking of instructional overload, the last day of instruction, a Thursday, finds me shooting as poorly as I ever have in my life. I mean I'm so bad that I would have difficulty breaking a target if it was suspended motionless at the end of a string ten feet in front of me. Dan Carlisle watches me whiff a few times at the "gliding grouse" station—a fast right-to-left ninety-degree

crossing bird, one of my weakest shots. "You're a bird hunter, right?" he asks.

"Yeah, kind of," I answer, filled with self-loathing.

"You haven't done much clay target shooting?"

"Not much." (In fact, my interest in shooting has always been quite specific to the field and I've never shot a full round of sporting clays until this week.)

"What you need to do," advises Carlisle, "is climb up on top of about a dozen cases of targets and shoot until you're standing on the ground again."

Sound advice to any shooter. Still, I'm not exactly thrilled, I can tell you, to have come this far, taken all this instruction, and shot more clays pigeons in a month than I have in my entire shooting life and currently be shooting worse than when I started out. Indeed, I'm in such a black funk about it that I'm seriously considering skipping tomorrow's tournament altogether; I feel like a cranky ten-year-old bad sport—I think I'll just pick up my marbles and go home.

Then as the last shooter at the last station on the last day of instruction I manage, under Roland Wild's calm tutelage, to break my final three birds; a good time to quit. "Those were the three best shots I've seen you make all week, Jim," says Roland, who, though suffering from a severe headache from having listened to roughly seven thousand shotgun blasts today (many of them from the obnoxiously loud "ported" guns of the Sporting Clays specialists), is still somehow able to maintain his enthusiasm, to make even the most hapless shooter feel a little better about himself.

Maybe there is some pressure for, say, the top three of four shooters in the school at large to shoot well in the tournament on this last day, to win, but for the vast majority of us, frankly, other than the personal satisfaction (some inkling of improve-

ment?), this isn't exactly the World Championships. It's sup-posed to be fun. Still, I had passed on that second martini at the cocktail party the evening before, I got a good night's sleep, went easy on the coffee this morning, and I am feeling pretty good. I'm glad to have Sheika on my team for the tournament. (It's impossible not to have fun shooting with her; at one station she keeps complaining that something is wrong, she's not seeing the target properly. Then it occurs to her, with a burst of raucous laughter, that she is shutting *both* her eyes before shooting.) And I'm pleased to have Roland as our coach; his relaxed style has a calming influence on me.

We are to shoot a total of 150 targets (10 at each station), with prizes to be awarded at the closing banquet that night for both the top three individual scores and the top three team scores. And a booby prize for low score. God, I just hope I don't win the booby prize.

The reader can only imagine how much I'd love here to relate an inspirational tale in which the Worst Shooter in America launches a miraculous comeback, starts dusting targets, shooting stronger and stronger throughout the day, working his way up to the lead and a climactic three-way shoot-off at the last station against, say, Gen. Norman Schwartzkopf and expert shotgunner Michael McIntosh, while the theme song from *Rocky* builds to a crescendo in the background.

But, of course, that is not precisely the way it happened. Ac-tually, the general had a bit of a lapse in concentration himself; later I learned that the State Department had called him the night before to inform him of intelligence reports of an Iranian hit team in the United States with orders to assassinate him. Even though shooting school with fifty armed students and a half-dozen instructors would seem to be a notably poor choice of places to make a hit, the news did put an understandable damper on the general's competitive spirit.

For his part, McIntosh finished in a very respectable third place. As for me, I didn't shoot badly, especially considering my

disastrous performance the day before. Sure, I missed my share of targets, and I suppose I finished (and our team, too) somewhere down around the middle of the pack, though I did win the sixteen-gauge class. (OK, so maybe I was the only person shooting a sixteen-gauge.)

But you know, all of a sudden I started feeling that gun stock coming right up to my cheek, just like it's supposed to, and when it did, even if I missed the bird, I didn't mind so much—because I *looked* good. And now that I'm mastering the technique, I'm actually entertaining a secret fantasy of going back next year . . . bringing my trusty bird gun again . . . what the hell . . . maybe winning the whole damn thing! Oh, my final score? Well, as an Anglophile bird hunter of my acquaintance once explained to me, the English have a saying: a gentleman only counts his change.

31

HACKERS

I have two sets of sporting buddies: my newer expert friends who do everything from bird shooting to fly casting to game cooking with almost infuriating perfection and grace, and my older, shall we say, less-expert friends, who like me—and let me put this as politely as possible—are strictly amateur sportsmen.

These latter are the guys I've been hunting and fishing with for some thirty years, long before I accidentally fell into the profession of "outdoor writer," which designation may falsely suggest that I actually possess some level of competence, even expertise in my chosen outdoor pursuits—a notion that by now has surely been put to rest once and for all.

I and my hacker buddies (of course, I use this term in the old sense of the word, not the modern computer usage of it) tend not to take ourselves too seriously, and in that spirit we often provide some comic relief for the real experts—and God knows that everyone, especially the experts, can benefit from lightening up a little. I mean, although the sporting life must be pursued with some modicum of respect and humility, it is not, as they

say, brain surgery. It is neither the answer to world peace, nor to world hunger It's supposed to be fun, the whole point simply to be out there, enjoying oneself. We do the best we can, but let's not feel a whole lot of pressure to be perfect. What I'm trying to say is: it's OK to be a hacker.

Which is not to say that the hacker doesn't try to improve himself. For my part, I've been working on various sporting self-improvement schemes all my life. One must have goals. At the same time, one must also learn to accept one's limitations. It has become painfully clear to me that I'm never going to be a tournament fly caster, or a great wing shot . . . all right, I'm not even going to be really good fly caster or wing shot. So I aspire to one day be slightly above average at both shooting and fly casting, a goal that seems to me to be realistically within reach.

In this same spirit of anticompetitiveness many years ago, my original hacker sporting buddies and I instituted a venerable tradition we call the "John Warner Award." So named after its original recipient, a crony, who forgot to bring his reel on a backcountry fishing trip many years ago, this award goes every year to that member of our party who commits the biggest blunder on our annual fishing or bird hunting trip. The idea is that not only excellence, but also gross incompetence should be recognized in our mutual sporting pursuits, for the fact is that in our group the goofs and the gaffes, the misses and the missteps, the boners and the bloopers are often more memorable, and certainly more reliable for future reference, than the occasional rare sporting triumph.

Since its inception, the John Warner Award has been presented for many, sometimes more and sometimes less serious screw-ups—everything from snapping rod tips in car doors, to forgetting to bring the food on wilderness camping trips, to locking the keys in the car in the middle of the Nebraska prairie, to showing up on an early morning pheasant hunt wearing a pair of fleece-lined bedroom slippers, to getting lost in the field, to falling in the river and nearly drowning, to hooking oneself

in the ear with a fly, to hooking one's buddy in the ear with a fly, to forgetting to take the safety off on an easy double, to arriving on a bird hunt and discovering that you've left your dog at home, to driving off and forgetting your dog in the field, to any number of Jerry Lewis-like pratfalls and mishaps. Really. The list of screw-ups, large and small, is endless, and over the years we've pretty much done it all.

Most years there is a clear, hands-down winner of the John Warner Award, though it seems like every year the competition gets fiercer, the standards for winning ever higher. This might suggest that as sportsmen, and even just as human beings, we are actually becoming more incompetent with the passage of time, but these days, merely forgetting one's reel would barely earn honorary mention.

Yet so refined has the competition also become these days that sometimes something as subtle as a particularly boneheaded remark will be enough to take home the coveted prize.

For instance, one year on a quail hunt in Arizona, our friends Jon Williams and David Christian became temporarily lost in the desert. They came across some cattle that Williams remembered seeing hours earlier. "Oh, good, we must be close to the vehicles," he said with relief, "there are the cows we saw earlier."

"Jon, you're a canny old desert rat," D. C. said, "but I must point out to you that cattle are known to move. Or, possibly these are different cattle altogether. Unless, of course, you happen to recognize one of them."

"Damn," said Williams, shaking his head. "I'm an idiot. Now not only are we probably going to get die in the desert, but I will have won the John Warner award."

Every year John Warner himself lobbies to have his name retired from our award, changed to that of the current winner. And every year, we explain to him that they don't change the name of the Nobel Prize each year, and that he should consider it a great honor to have our award named after him. And every year Warner says, "This isn't exactly the Nobel Prize, is it?"

Well, no it isn't. And some inevitable day, when one of us makes a really, *really* big mistake, I'm talking a monumental FUCK-UP—actually dying in the desert, say—then we might actually consider retiring the John Warner Award for all time.

In fact, on our last annual summer fishing trip I came rather close to doing just that myself. And it wasn't even a sporting mishap, but a cooking accident, which counts in our competition, because sport and cooking are so inextricably intertwined. (On occasion the award has gone to someone just for preparing a particularly bad meal.)

In this case, I was in the process of lighting the oven in the Airstream before dinner, when distracted by some kitchen chore or other, I evidently forgot that I'd already turned the pilot on a few minutes earlier, but had neglected to light it. Now I opened the door of the oven, and just as the scent of gas reached my nostrils a millisecond too late for me to register that I was about to incinerate myself, I struck the match and was immediately engulfed by a whooshing fireball of flame. God, what an incredibly lame thing to do!

The boys looked down at me, kneeling by the oven, regarding the singed hairs on my arm, shaking my head and trying to assess the damage as the acrid scent of scorched hair filled the air. "Aw, *shit*," I muttered.

"Looks like your eyebrows are toast," one of them said, "but you still have most of the hair on your head."

"And you're not dead," another added.

"Better yet, we're not all dead," a third said.

"But guess what, buddy?" someone asked.

"Yeah, yeah, I know," I answered. "And the winner is . . ."

32

STATE OF GRACE

It was a hot summer day and I was fishing alone on a remote lower stretch of Wyoming's North Platte River. The river here has long since left the mountains, left the irrigated hay fields of the valley behind, and dropped down into country that is essentially desert. There are rattlesnakes in this country—in fact, I had rarely fished it or camped here without seeing at least one rattler. I'm not ashamed to admit that I don't like rattlesnakes. I don't exactly have a snake phobia, but at the same time you'll never catch me signing on with one of those snake-handling religious sects, either. Yet though I have had a few close encounters with snakes on this stretch of the river, I still come here to fish from time to time because it is a beautiful piece of water, worth facing one's fears for.

Any people who spend any time at all in the outdoors (and by that I don't mean sitting around the barbecue on the deck) will find themselves in a tight spots now and again (and by that I don't mean, "Honey, I've overcooked the steaks again!"). And one of the qualities that I've always admired most in outdoors-

men and always hoped to cultivate myself is the ability to get out of a tight spot with dignity, skill, and confidence. Hemingway defined this quality as "grace under pressure," but I'm also talking about simple competence, which is sometimes much the same thing. In fact, being competent and/or graceful in the outdoors often allows one to avoid tight spots altogether.

I grew up in the suburbs reading the outdoor magazines and dreaming of this sporting life. Those guys could do it all, and do it well. They were great shots and great anglers; they could start a fire and navigate by compass; they knew the habits of the fish and birds and mammals; they knew how to take care of themselves in the outdoors. And they knew how to get out of a tight spot.

All these years later, I'm not even going to pretend that I'm especially competent in the outdoors, and certainly not all that graceful. Not that I'm a total *klutz*, but if, for instance, there is a barbwire fence within half a mile of me, chances are that I will snag my waders on it. When I was a kid, my mother always used to say that I was a bit "vague" and my father said that I'd "lose my head if it wasn't screwed on." I was a dreamer, still am, which is not a quality that is conducive to real competence in the outdoors.

And I wonder now if perhaps the general tone of my outdoor life wasn't set way back then by a single galvanizing event of childhood. I was ten or eleven years old and had been invited by my best friend's family on a wilderness canoe trip. On the very first day, the very first stretch of white water, I lurched awkwardly and tipped over the canoe. My friend's mother was pitched out, broke her leg on a rock, and had to be airlifted to the hospital. My best friend's mom. Her leg snapped like a twig.

Ever since that experience a large measure of my interest in the sporting life has been fueled by the largely unrealized search for grace, competence—to be a better wing shot, a better fly caster, to be the kind of guy who doesn't capsize the canoe and with whom you wouldn't mind being lost in the woods. (Hey,

I've been lost with me in the woods countless times, and I can promise you, it's no picnic.) Guys like my old friend and mentor, Barney Donnelley.

One time, some years ago, Barney and I were caught in his fishing boat in a sudden squall off the coast of Florida. We were running for the inlet when the maelstrom of wind and rain overtook us. The sea and air went strangely black as huge twenty-foot swells crashed over the bow. Barney told me to lie down in the bow and hang on while he manned the wheel. I admit I was terrified, but I had complete confidence in Donnelley; I knew he would pull us through, for he possessed that ineffable quality of grace under pressure, without which I'm convinced we would have perished out there on the high seas.

And last year on a high, runoff-swollen river in Montana, Donnelley, though now in his sixties, saved the life of a younger, inexperienced fishing companion who had been swept off his feet by the current. As the man floated downriver, he desperately reached his fly rod out to Barney, who managed to grab hold of the tip. But the man had reeled his fly up to the end of the rod, as only beginners will do, and it embedded itself to the shank into Donnelley's palm. Still he held on and dragged the man, half as young and half again as heavy as he, to the safety of shore before losing his own footing and being swept away, very nearly drowning himself.

Which brings me back to my tale: It was midday and hot, and although I should have been laying up in the shade somewhere, instead I was fishing a favorite deep pool with a wet fly and a sinking line on the theory that whatever fish were in this stretch of river would be right down on the bottom. I knew this pool well, and I'd waded out carefully to within about an inch of the top of my chest waders. I was standing on a small rock, my footing a bit precarious to be sure, but in order to reach the part of the pool where the fish were holed up, this was where I needed to be.

I cast down and across, mending my line while the fly sank,

then let the line "belly" in the current to sweep the fly through the pool. When the line straightened out downstream I began my retrieve. On my very first strip a fish hit—a solid take, a good fish.

The trout bulled upstream, stripping line from the reel. I played him carefully for several minutes until he began to tire. At about this point, out of the corner of my eye I caught sight of something on the water floating down toward me. I looked more carefully and realized with astonishment—well, horror actually—that it was a rattlesnake; its body describing a series of loose "s" curves on the water's surface, the rattler seemed to be taking a leisurely ride down the river, cooling off in the heat of the day. What's more, it was floating right at me, on a direct collision course, and seemed entirely oblivious to my presence.

A number of thoughts raced through my mind: First, with the river so close to the top of my waders, I knew that there was no hope of maneuvering out of the snake's way without losing my footing and being swept away by the current. So I appeared to have a choice between drowning and becoming entangled with the snake. Worst case scenario: I was going to get bit by the rattlesnake—and because only my chest, neck, and head were above water I was going to get bit in a real bad place—and then I was going to drown.

I still had the fish on, my right arm raised with the rod in hand, and there was really nothing to do but freeze, which I did, an involuntary reaction at that. Possibly I whispered, "Hey, Mr. Snake?" just to alert it to the impending collision, because just then it saw me and scooted with incredible dexterity, as if it were on solid land and not water, a couple of feet to the side. It's true, snakes can walk on water. Now it raised its head up off the water like a snake charmer's pet and turned to face me as it floated past, no more than eighteen inches away, looking at me at eye level and flicking its tongue in warning. I did not move. I won't say that my whole life flashed before my eyes in that moment, but for some odd reason I had the clearest memory

of kissing Charlotte Goodwin on a park bench when I was sixteen years old.

The snake and I looked each other right in the eye as it floated past and in that instant we made our deal. It continued on its float downriver, and I landed the trout, a beautiful eighteen-inch rainbow that I released back to the water.

33

ZEN AND THE ART
OF NYMPH FISHING

My friend Rob Kelly has been fishing Aspen's fabled Roaring
Fork River long before the river was even fabled, long before
Aspen had become the glittering "Hollywood of the West" that
we know it as today. Since he was a youth, his family has owned
a modest little vacation home in the heart of town, the kind of
house that realtors refer to these days as a "scraper"—the lot,
small as it is, far more valuable than the house itself. Most of
the Kellys' old neighbors have long since caved into the relentless financial incentives of a real estate market gone mad, their
once equally modest homes bulldozed to make way for huge,
ungainly trophy homes that occupy every square inch of available lot space—which gives these new monstrosities somewhat
the look of elephants perched on stools. The Kellys' house
crouches bravely among them, the last vestige of another, less
ostentatious time.

But some things never change, and as it always has the Roaring Fork River runs right through Aspen, right beneath the Kel-

lys' house, and here in its higher reaches, it is a very different river than it is further downstream. Here at the base of the mountains, the river has formed a series of deep, boulder-lined pools that spill into one another.

Carrying our waders and rods, we walk down the neighborhood sidewalk to access Rob Kelly's local stretch of the river—past the Meadows tennis courts, past the gazebos and hot tubs, over the lawns of multimillion-dollar houses belonging to lucky families from Los Angeles, and on down to the river.

A path, actually a paved sidewalk, with strategically spaced benches along its length, follows the Roaring Fork through town, offering a convenient and scenic corridor for runners, walkers, bicyclists, and rollerbladers—and, not incidentally, anglers. However, most people who fish the river tend to do so further downstream, past Slaughterhouse Bridge where the Roaring Fork has carved a deep canyon, or further downstream yet towards Basalt, or in the floatable meadow stretches between Carbondale and Glenwood Springs.

But this "urban" stretch of the river is Kelly's domain—his home water. He knows every pool and every boulder. He knows where to enter each of the deep holes, where to step from rock to rock in order to get to his optimum fishing station without going in over the top of his waders. And he knows many of the trout who reside here personally.

Before we start fishing we take a seat on a bench overlooking the Roaring Fork, which makes a noise like the bass section of an orchestra, less a roar than a kind of deep, steady rumble, punctuated by the lighter, faster tones of riffles and falls. It's a cool midsummer morning and the cottonwood along the river are a deep shade of green and rustle ever so slightly in the faint breeze.

Waders draped across his lap, Kelly leans forward and stares intently at the river and seems to enter a kind of Zen state, as if trying to penetrate the surface of the water, to decipher in the depths of the pool its darkest secrets.

"What are we doing?" I finally ask.

Just then a pair of what can only be Hollywood trophy wives clad in tight spandex pants and sports bras jog past. Bodies sculpted by personal trainers, and quite possibly nipped and tucked here and there by artful plastic surgeons, they are improbably idealized specimens of the human race. But then Aspen itself is an improbably idealized specimen of an old mining town.

"Ogling babes," Kelly says, "It's one of the advantages of fishing in town. And we're also watching the water. Put your waders on now. I'll take this pool, you take the next one up. From here on we have to creep. Make as little noise and disturbance as possible. Pretend you're an emerging nymph."

"An emerging nymph?"

But Rob has already slipped quietly into his waders and is moving stealthily as a cat burglar down the path to the river. I decide that I'd better watch him for a while, try to pick up some pointers. Kelly is a master of the technique of short-line nymph fishing. I've never really had the requisite Zenlike patience for it myself.

Crouched slightly, holding his rod in hand like a conductor's baton, Kelly enters the pool and works his way very slowly and carefully into position near its center. Then he just stands there, motionless as a statue, until he has become a part of the structure of the river itself, and the pool has settled and the fish that he has disturbed upon entrance take up their feeding stations again. Then he works out a little line, and I mean a little, and begins to cast upstream. Actually "cast" isn't exactly the right word; using a twist-on lead sinker on a short leader he kind of "flips" his bead-head green caddis upstream. With the weight, the fly sinks quickly. Crouched in an attitude of total concentration, Kelly holds his pole aloft as delicately as if he is wielding a divining rod, staring intently at his line as the fly bumps along the bottom of the pool. Every now and then he makes a short hook-setting motion, just a gentle flick of his wrist; so delicately do trout pick up the nymphs, that's it's often impossible, even

for the Master, to differentiate between an actual strike and the fly just bumping the bottom. At the end of the drift he picks up, and begins the same sequence all over again. Every fifth or sixth drift he checks his fly for weed or moss.

Watching the process from my bench is somehow soothing, nearly hypnotic, and I am in no particular hurry to begin fishing myself. Plus I can ogle babes passing on the sidewalk before me—joggers and fast walkers and rollerbladers—a river of spandex flowing alongside the actual river.

Flip, follow drift, pick-up, flip, with the patience of a Benedictine monk saying repetitive liturgies, Kelly works the pool over and over again. He will stay in one pool for as long as an hour. And his patience will be rewarded; he will catch fish, and big ones.

After Kelly hooks his first trout, his rod arced and throbbing, and lands a fat brown, which he releases back to the water, I finally leave my place on the bench and creep downstream to try my hand in the next pool. But try as I might to imitate Kelly, even adopting his hunched posture and his habit of humming, which he does much as a Buddhist chants, I never catch as many, or as big a fish as he does. It's simply not in my nature to be so methodical, so calm and repetitive and patient. But I keep trying nevertheless, hoping to learn from the Master, for as the Buddhists say, "The path is the way."

34

THE END OF THE SEASON

It was a late-fall afternoon and we were fishing a high plains lake full of fat rainbows and "cutbows" (a rainbow/cutthroat hybrid). The trout had been gorging all summer on freshwater shrimp, and their flesh was as pink as salmon. But this time of day—just as the sun was setting and the light had gone silvery and the last hatches of the season were on—the fish sometimes started feeding on the surface, rolling lazily like porpoises, their top fins and tails breaking the water. It was something to see, I can tell you—a big six-pounder cruising along just under the surface, leaving a wake like a submarine until he spotted something to eat—hopefully your fly—and rolled slowly, languidly, his back humping out of the water as he sipped delicately, the disturbance on the still surface looking and sounding like the suction swirl when the bathtub drain plug is pulled.

I had decided to climb to the crest of a small hill overlooking the lake, due to the spectacular vantage point it offered and because, frankly, Sweetz, had grown bored now with fishing. She had been sitting on the bank all summer watching patiently as

I fished, but now it was fall again and she thought we should be doing something else . . . hunting, for instance. And I kind of had to agree with her; I was a little tired of fishing myself, and although I hesitate to complain about catching five-pound-plus trout all summer long in a spectacular, secret high plains lake, I must admit that I'd reached that stage of the season where I'd just as soon watch from this vantage point as my old friends Jon and John fished.

So Sweetz and I noodled about in the sagebrush atop the hill; maybe we'd even flush some sage grouse up here, though currently I was carrying a fly rod rather than a shotgun and wearing neoprene waders rather than brush pants.

We had hunted earlier in the day (this was the "boys'" annual "cast and blast" weekend) and had gotten into a covey of sage grouse in the flats. Dinner had been procured. This evening we fished; tomorrow we'd probably hunt the blue grouse in the mountains.

It had been a dry summer, and down below the mowed hay meadows had turned various shades of tan and brown and ocher, while the sage-dotted hills around were tawny and reddish with the setting sun. The willows along the ditches and creek bottoms were yellow, their leaves already spiraling to the ground like tiny parachutes. Bunches of cows peppered the landscape, and it occurred to me standing up here that though cattle are getting a lot of bad press recently, I'd rather have them in this picture than the ubiquitous housing developments that seem to be eating up the West these days.

Down below, Jon and John stood waist-deep in the water on opposite sides of the small lake, casting rhythmically, the last bit of afternoon sunlight sparking off their lines. We were all old friends—the best kind—had known each other virtually all of our adult lives, and will be cronies to the grave.

I suppose because I spend so much time these days on the road, I particularly cherish these rare moments at home with my old friends. Later we'd all cook dinner together; we'd squabble

around the kitchen like a bunch of little old ladies: John would be accused of not bringing his fair share of supplies, and the story would be retold of the Thanksgiving a dozen years ago when he showed up with exactly one can of candied yams as his contribution to dinner. I would be accused of being overly bossy and excessively fastidious. Jon would be accused of drinking all the red wine before we even sat down to dinner. And, what's more, all of these accusations would be true. Indeed, we'd all drink too much; we'd smoke, though really we'd all given it up years ago; we'd compare gray hairs and receding hairlines; we'd catch up on one another's latest physical ailments—a laugh-infested litany of middle-age decrepitude. (We are not so old that these things don't still astonish us.) But dinner, I could almost guarantee, would be excellent—grilled first-year sage grouse that we shot this morning, wild rice, a green salad, fresh French bread . . .

But I'm getting ahead of myself again. Just at that moment it was still the tail end of the fishing season, a season come and gone, and another about to take its place, in the endless cycle of this sporting life. Indeed, in just a few days I would be hooking up the Airstream and leaving home once again with Sweetz on our annual fall migration.

Right now I was watching from atop the hill as my old friend Jon made a particularly good cast—his loop unfurling perfectly, his fly dropping gracefully, eighteen inches or so ahead of a cruising trout. I watched as the big fish spotted this new offering and accelerated ever so slightly to reach it—his huge hooked jaw breaking the surface like a claw, his dark mottled back rolling as if in slow motion out of the water, his bright side flashing in the day's last light.

Ever since I've known him, Jon has had a tendency to be a split second slow on the strike; we've teased him relentlessly over the years about this angling shortcoming. "Got one!" he always hollered on the take. "Lost him," he says, crestfallen, in the next breath.

But this time he lifted his rod tip just at the right moment and set the hook. "Got one!" he hollered, triumphant. And his line straightened and his rod arced and his reel began to sing. And I had the best seat in the house.

EPILOGUE

Where the Seasons Go

Years are terrible things.

 —Zane Grey, *Riders of the Purple Sage*

I don't know where the seasons go, but they go by fast—don't they?—each seeming to accelerate through the next like a New York City taxicab hitting the green lights just right at dawn on Park Avenue, one block blurring into the next and the next and the next after that . . . .

Somehow it's September again as I write this, another bird season already under way. Sweetz is growing old now; she'll turn ten next month. Her elbows are as scarred by surgeries as the knees of a retired professional quarterback; in fact, her whole body is like a road map of our sporting life together, her pads worn thin from thousands of miles in the rocky hills and the mountains and the desert and the prairie, her belly and chest

scarred by barbwire, cacti, thorns, and briers. She moves stiffly now, with little of the lionesslike grace of her youth, and the hair around her muzzle is whitening with age, her eyes beginning to cloud over. But she's still good for a couple of hours' hunt, and she can still find birds. Maybe this will be her last hunting season, or maybe she has one more left in her. . . . Each year, that's all we ask for: one more season.

Last year Sweetz and I took on a new young upstart named Henri, a French Brittany from the famed Calembour/Dogwood line (though we are not so effete as to pronounce his name in the French manner). Sweetz has shown Henri a thing or two; she found and flushed a covey of sage grouse in front of him back home in Colorado when he was just five months old. You could see the lightbulb go off in his little puppy brain, and when I killed a brace of birds he went berserk for their scent, though they were bigger than he was and he couldn't pick them up. The next time we went out, Henri winded the birds himself, at least two hundred yards out, and off he went to flush a huge covey and chase them for another half-mile. That's OK; he was just a puppy and did not know yet that he was a pointing dog.

The next month in Washington State, Henri, Sweetzer, and I hunted chukars, Huns, pheasants, and California quail. Henri made a couple of nice retrieves, once stealing a chukar right out of the mouth of one of my friend Rick Bass's exuberant German shorthairs, named Pointman and Superman, respectively. Still, Henri showed no inclination to point.

It wasn't until the month after that, November, when we got down to my friend Guy de la Valdène's Dogwood Farm, where Henri had been born eight months earlier, that his pointing dog genes kicked in. The very first morning we went out to hunt bobwhite quail, he locked up on a covey as if he'd been doing it all his life, and all of a sudden Sweetzer and I both understood why we had endured Henri's monstrous puppy behavior these past months. The little twerp could find birds for us. All was forgiven.

But, of course, this is not Henri's story, this is Sweetzer's story, and now it's coming to an end. I don't know where the seasons have gone, but I do know that there's no sense in getting sentimental or weepy about it. I have drawn the map of our sporting life in yellow highlighter on countless dog-eared road atlases over the years, and the tale the map tells is an endless dream of birds and country and friends, new and old. What a fine life Sweetz and I have had together, and still have. How much country we have seen in each other's company, with more yet to see. How truly lucky we have been, and are. And now the season begins anew; the Suburban is warming up in the driveway, the Airstream hooked up and ready to roll—its running lights glowing like those of a wingless aircraft in the milky light of dawn . . . May all hunters and their dogs be so graced. Good hunting.

Rand, Colorado
September 1998